CHOOSING A MAJOR

RESPECTING DIVERSITY

TIME MANAGEMENT

COMMUNICATING

MAINTAINING WELLNESS

LIFE LESSONS 101

NAVIGATING THE UNWRITTEN COURSE OF COLLEGE

Stella Erbes

Kendall Hunt
publishing company

Cover image © Shutterstock.com; Natalie Myers, Hong Kha, & Landon Phillips

Kendall Hunt
publishing company

www.kendallhunt.com
Send all inquiries to:
4050 Westmark Drive
Dubuque, IA 52004-1840

This book is dedicated to

Richard, my love,

and

Josh and Jacob, my legacies.

Contents

Acknowledgments

I am sincerely grateful to many key people who have assisted me throughout the journey of writing of this book. From conception to conclusion, I was fortunate to have a network of talented resources to support and guide me with writing, editing, and publishing. A familiar African proverb states, "It takes a village to raise a child," and the same wisdom applies to raising an author. I acknowledge the members of my village here, and extend my deepest gratitude for all the time and talent they have shared with me to bring this book to fruition.

I am extremely thankful for my acquisitions editor, Matt Lozano, who shared my vision to make this resource available to college students and opened the door to make this book a reality. A special thanks also goes to Rachel Guhin and the Kendall-Hunt Publishing Company for their utmost professionalism, keen insights, and numerous talents.

I acknowledge that my life and my work are a testament of my family, who relentlessly invested in me and shaped who I am today. To my grandmother ("Harmony"), whose wisdom and spirit have sustained me throughout my life, thank you for teaching me some of my greatest life lessons, which I continue to apply in and out of my classroom. To my mother and father, who are my examples of courage and commitment, I thank you for teaching me that there are no boundaries to what I can accomplish. To my big brother, John, and my sister-in-love, Arlene, thank you for continuously inspiring me to dream a bigger dream and never letting me doubt that I can realize my goals.

To my loving and supportive husband, Richard, thank you for faithfully supporting me in all that I do. I always tell my students that everyone needs a cheerleader; thank you for always being mine. To my dear sons, Josh and Jacob, I am grateful for the unconditional love that we share and the many life lessons that we have learned together. It is an honor to be your mother.

Thank you to all my loyal friends and special students who graciously invested their time to read and revise drafts of this manuscript and contribute creatively to the project: Rahje Branch, Beau Brannan, Jenessa Bryant, Jessie Burns, Sarah Dalton, Dakota Duffy, Grace Fitzgerald, Dr. Kristen Chiem, Carol Hartnett, Dr. Jennifer Johnson, Hong Kha, Caeli Koizumi, Davina Morales, Tara Morrow, Josh Myers, Landon Phillips, Teresa Roberson, Tatum Shackelford, Jane Tsang, Lisa Wayne, Maggie Weiss, Emma Woods, and Elizabeth Yomantas. I am confident that this book is more polished because of all of your efforts.

A special thanks to a host of prayer warriors, whose encouraging words and positive thoughts inspired me during this project: Al and Dorothy Aulwurm, Michaela Carrera, Allie Davis, Bill Denzel, Dr. Michael Ditmore, Emily Dilbeck, Dr. Connie Fulmer, Claudia Joensuu,

Wendi Klaiber, Matthew Linden, Frank and Teresa Myers, and my "sisters," Kayla Chao, Aimee Denzel, and Ann Suk Wang.

To special angels, such as Bill and Rhonni Greig, Amos Bracero and David Exline, and Risa and Tyrrell Erbes, who provided a quiet refuge for me to retreat to so that I could complete my writing—thank you for your incredible hospitality, your encouraging prayers, and your unending support.

It is with a grateful heart that I acknowledge these individuals and the various ways that they have sustained me throughout my journey of life lessons.

Introduction

Congratulations! You are about to begin one of the most formative experiences of your life as a college student. Beyond the academic knowledge that will expand your intellectual curiosity, this journey offers implicit and explicit life lessons that will ultimately shape you. The distinctive experience of college life is exclusive to a small percentage of the nation. Although people tend to assume that the majority of high school graduates continue their studies in higher education, the modest number of students who choose to pursue a degree at the university level is rather surprising. The U.S. Department of Commerce (2015) reported that only 40 percent of 18–24-year-olds enrolled in college in 2014, which was merely 0.5 percent higher than in 2000. For some of you, the decision to attend college was a given; this was your family's clear expectation since you were a child, and the thought of foregoing higher learning was not an option. On the contrary, a number of freshmen come from backgrounds where they have defied the odds and have overcome numerous obstacles to break the barriers that have historically deterred their family members from attending college; you represent the first-generation student. No matter what your journey to this point has entailed, you have answered the call, and as a college student, you are about to embark on an incredible, unique path into adulthood that will transform you in boundless ways.

The college journey initiates a time of tremendous personal growth that stems from learning life lessons that promote social, moral, sexual, ethical, spiritual, intellectual, and professional development. This unofficial curriculum often supersedes the content knowledge gained in traditional classrooms. College students do not formally register for a class that explicitly teaches life lessons. This is the unwritten course of college that accompanies students as they live independently, reflect deeply, and choose carefully how to respond to and manage all the dimensions of these formative years of development. This text equips undergraduates with practical strategies and tools to help them navigate the life lessons learned in college.

Having taught a first-year seminar for six years and mentored college students for fifteen years, I have seen patterns of behavior in the development of undergraduates, and I have documented skills and lessons that have been valuable to them for their success. A plethora of questions immediately bombard students' minds as they begin college. Initially, a typical set of questions addresses the basic structures of university life and usually includes the following:

1. What is your major? What career do you want to pursue?
2. Who is your roommate? What is he/she like?
3. Will you study abroad?
4. Will you join a Greek organization or a particular club?
5. Will you work or complete an internship?

After students assimilate into the culture of higher education, other questions that deal with personal and professional development arise:

6. What is your vocation or your calling in life?
7. How will you communicate professionally with college professors, administration, staff, or future employers?
8. How will you resolve conflict with roommates or professors?
9. How will you thrive as a student? (e.g., time management and studying)
10. Will you continue to practice your faith as a college student? Or will you explore or consider other faith traditions?
11. How will you develop your research, writing, and presentation skills?
12. What will you do after graduation?

First-year seminars are intended to guide students as they grapple with the answers to these questions, in addition to exposing students to a professor's special field of interest (e.g., literature, sciences, or education). However, it is typical for first-year seminars to function without a common text for classes to address these vital questions. Freshmen and transfer students would benefit from a shared resource that would allow all new members of the college community to reflect upon the same core of life lessons. Also, in universities where first-year seminars are not offered and do not address this aspect of adult development, mentoring groups, students clubs, or residential halls could adopt this reflective guide to help support college students to successfully navigate these life lessons. It is my hope that this text will serve as a handbook for students to follow as they build a repertoire of skills needed to thrive in college and beyond.

How is the college experience unique?

The college years are unlike the traditional experiences of primary and secondary schools. This is one of the most shocking realizations for first-year college students as they enter this new phase of life. At first glance, the average college class schedule appears fairly easy and sparse when compared to the stressful, rigorous daily schedule of high school. Instead of attending classes each school day for six consecutive hours, classes meet less frequently, and there are large gaps of time in students' schedules and more freedom to take naps, schedule in work hours, or socialize during the day. ***This is a trap.*** One of the first life lessons that students face is priority management; they must learn how to successfully and purposefully plan their time.

College is not simply about taking courses, getting good grades, and earning a degree. The challenge in college is to complete all of these aforementioned tasks while independently—and simultaneously—managing relationships, monitoring finances, preserving mental and physical wellness, setting priorities, resolving conflict, and cultivating community. This is the unwritten curriculum of college that is commonly overlooked, yet requires immeasurable energy, tenacity, and grit. When learned successfully, these are the life lessons that will develop your adult character and will help you to become the best version of yourself in and out of the classroom.

College: Residential learning launches immediate growth

First, the college experience is immediately different for those who are not living at home or nearby family. Entering college as residential students, whether on or off-campus, plunges students into a world of independence that they never experienced while living at home. This aspect of college triggers prompt growth or painful stagnation. Some will thrive as they begin to function independently, while others will struggle to accomplish tasks on their own daily. The initial step of separating physically from one's home and family and living in a new community immediately prompts students to reflect upon their origins, both literally and figuratively, and initiates the formation of their independence and self-identities. The residential aspect of college sets this form of schooling apart from what most students have experienced previously, and this inherently launches students in their first step to living independently and forging their own way into adulthood.

Second, physical distance is a visible step toward independence. University students must quickly learn to assume responsibilities, which may have been shared before with caregivers at home. Some students may have already begun to cultivate this sense of independence before arriving at college, but now, they must navigate how to carry out these tasks away from their families in a communal, public space, such as their college dormitory or apartment, with people who do not know them as intimately. The shelter of comfort that living at home offered may have been unacknowledged before, but moving away from family catapults students into independent living, which helps students recognize the luxuries of home that may have once been taken for granted. These comforts include, but are not limited to, assistance with daily chores such as cleaning, laundry, and meal preparations, as well as caregiving tasks, such as preserving wellness through effective time management and protecting sleep or resting patterns. Being a part of a residential learning community offers many conveniences, but also many conflicts. Living in small spaces with people who are not (or sometimes, even *are*) family members opens the door to a myriad of potential disagreements and misunderstandings. This, combined with not having a quiet refuge to retreat to and recharge, especially for introverts, is particularly grueling. Managing new responsibilities independently and identifying methods to thrive in the tight quarters of a residential learning community, are life lessons that students encounter early on in their college experiences.

Lastly, the potential for personal growth and character development is great in the university setting. When one steps back to consider the unique infrastructure of college, it sets up a fascinating, experimental setting to gather empirical research for human behavior. Young adults are separated from their families, leave the comforts of their homes, are assigned to live with strangers in close quarters, must learn to navigate the foreign culture of college as well as their new surroundings, must digest difficult course content, and then, are tested about their knowledge of the material under stressful conditions. They must do all of this while simultaneously exploring their sexuality, reflecting upon their personal faith, being tempted by drugs and alcohol, and making life choices that will affect their futures. Personal growth under these tumultuous conditions is inevitable. The college environment is a jungle filled with challenging lessons that are difficult to navigate independently. Thus, the stage is set for learning some of life's most important lessons.

College: Welcome to a world of choices

Institutions of higher education open a new pathway to independence in both academic and human development. College marks the first time when education is not compulsory in legal terms, and students are given the freedom to select their discipline of study. Earning a college degree is much more than simply completing the required courses of a set curriculum, as TK-12 education programs have dictated. The undergraduate experience introduces students to a world of new, independent choices and launches them into adult development.

Academic Choices

Traditionally, children matriculate into the institution of education at the kindergarten level, or now even in TK, where teachers must adhere to a strict standards-based education. There is minimal choice given to students to select their courses until middle school when options for world languages or visual and performing arts are made available. High school students then work toward completing the requirements for a diploma, and a subset of that group simultaneously considers taking courses that will make their applications competitive in the college admission process. Academic choices in the TK-12 setting are limited and systematically follow a chronological sequence that accurately reflects the developmental philosophy of Jean Piaget, which states that students move through a series of stages (Woolfolk, 2016). For example, while attending elementary school, students focus on the fundamental skills of reading and writing and are introduced to socialization. Primary students will eventually graduate and move on to middle school, where they will begin to hone their skills developmentally to understand more abstract lessons. Subsequently, middle school students will advance to high school, where they will cultivate their critical thinking skills, learn to balance extracurricular activities with their academic load, and begin to prepare for what lies ahead for them after high school.

During these TK-12 years, however, students do not have to think of what the subsequent step is in their schooling. The next step is automatically set up for them in the educational system. Elementary school students move on to middle school, and then, middle school students advance to high school. Aside from the different tracks of classes offered (e.g., general, college preparatory, or Advanced Placement, etc.), there is little room for choice in the academic curriculum of TK-12 schooling. Students are conditioned to check off the standards or classes taken in one year, and they routinely move on to the next year.

Unlike the TK-12 curriculum, the college class schedule promotes independence and autonomy. Academically, students are given the responsibility to choose their own classes. If they do not enjoy their selected major, they may elect to change majors. Students do not attend each class daily, as they may be accustomed to from their secondary schooling, and they are able to select what classes to take and at what time of day. The weekly course schedule allows for ample breaks and free time. Moreover, students have the freedom to choose whether they attend classes or not. With this freedom of choice comes a responsibility to design one's college plan and manage one's time responsibly. Additionally, earning one's degree is not as simple as merely checking off the academic coursework each year as students were used to doing in high school. Along with the academic curriculum of college come the life lessons of these developmental years, and this is what makes learning in higher education so much more than the consumption of content knowledge.

Life Choices

In addition to being introduced to the freedom to make choices in their academic careers, college students also enter a time in their lives when they are independently making life choices. Some of these decisions may be as simple as when to go to bed or whether to attend class or not, while others may be more complex, such as exploring drug or alcohol use or being sexually active. Discovering the impact of these life choices can be jolting and difficult, but from the pain comes growth.

I generally see that the college admissions team at my university has done an excellent job in selecting students with high academic achievements and strong qualities to succeed in college. The students that I teach have been accepted into a prestigious four-year university. In 2016, the university where I teach received over 11,000 applications, and a little less than 900 were accepted. These are exceptional students. However, once the challenges of living independently surface, these exemplary students are shaken. Sometimes, they do not rise to the same standards to which they were accustomed to when they lived at home, where they benefitted from the support of family and close friends nearby while navigating a traditional school schedule. Clearly, they have the potential to earn high grades in college, but often, their grades do not represent their academic abilities.

This conflict that college students encounter leads to many tears and much self-reflection. They are discovering that college is not just about going through the motions of checking off coursework and carrying on the same academic standards which they were accustomed to in high school. The curve ball that they were thrown lies in navigating the life lessons while simultaneously being a successful student. Acknowledgement of the self-growth produced from learning from the benefits and downfalls of the life choices you make in college is what this text makes visible. With freedom comes responsibility. The freedom is given; the responsibility is learned.

Make good choices, don't do drugs, stay in school

In January 2017, Former First Lady Michelle Obama addressed young people in her final public speech, encouraging them to equip themselves with the skills and education necessary "to build a country worthy of boundless promise." Colleges are filled with young people who are inspired, motivated, and eager to learn how to grow into the best version of themselves. The life lessons outlined in this text are intended to prepare students with the skills necessary to thrive, while navigating their college years and when working in professional environments thereafter. It is my hope that these life lessons will help shape mindful and healthy future leaders, who are effective communicators, charismatic presenters, empathetic listeners, and informed citizens who will prepare not only to live in our world, but give back to it.

It is now time to begin your college journey. You have been selected from a pool of thousands to live out this opportunity at your chosen university. You have been set apart from multitudes because you have earned the honor to engage in the college experience. As you enter into a developmental stage where you learn to navigate your way independently as a student and an adult, remember that this academic experience is unlike the traditional schooling that you have experienced before. This is your initiation into adulthood, a time where your choices will begin to build your professional resume and shape your personal character. Here, you will learn, grow, study, explore, and travel, so seize the moments that allow you to do all these things well.

In my own family, when my sons left the house for any occasion, we have routinely repeated this mantra, "Make good choices, don't do drugs, stay in school." They are simple words, but they cover the bases and subtly ensure success for their futures. So, I charge you all to do the same. *Make good choices.* Learn from the bad ones. Press on, even when you think you do not have the capacity to do so. Call your family regularly. Don't text, email, call, or talk to anyone while you are angry. Serve others. Don't let your mistakes define you. *Don't do drugs.* Sleep well. Eat healthy. Exercise daily. *Stay in school.* Keep up with your readings. Be open to teachable moments, both in and out of the classroom. Study abroad or travel as much as you can. Find a mentor. And, enjoy the journey.

CHAPTER 1

Major, Career, and Vocation

"What Is Your Major?" and Other Life-Determining Questions

> "True vocation is the place where your deep gladness meets the world's deep need."
>
> — *Frederick Buechner*

Once you declare yourself as a college student, a set of automatic questions will follow. These questions routinely include the following:

1. What is your major?
2. What career path have you chosen?
3. Why do you want to do that?

Our society has conditioned itself to ask college students to respond articulately to these life-changing, transformative questions. It boggles my mind that people assume that college freshmen, who are 17–18 years old, will already have decided what they want to study for the next four years of their lives before even experiencing a college campus firsthand or considering all the majors that are available. On rare occasions, some students have committed to a particular professional pathway, such as becoming a doctor or a teacher early on in their college careers, but the National Center for Education Statistics indicated that 80 percent of college students change their majors at least once, and on average, students change their major three times during their collegiate career (Ramos, 2013). Whether students have confidently decided on a major area of study or not, there are some points that all college students should carefully consider as they select their major and make plans for their career goals. This chapter will present guidelines to consider when choosing a major, picking a career path, and discovering one's vocation.

Choosing a major—step #1: Assess your strengths, weaknesses, and interests

Before arriving at college, students usually select a major based upon an assessment of their own strengths and interests. It is helpful to pause and complete a self-inventory of strengths and weaknesses as a student in order to understand better what courses and careers are viable options. For instance, if a student is shy and timid when giving public presentations, then a major in the Communications field is, most likely, unrealistic. However, if a student thrives on classic novels, then researching the English major or the Great Books course sequence could merit further investigation. Even if students are uncertain about what types of classes they firmly like, they are typically confident about what areas of study they do *not* like. For example, a student may be open to exploring diverse history courses, but may vehemently detest math courses. As a result, by completing a self-inventory of personal interests, initial steps can easily be taken to begin whittling down the multitude of possibilities of academic majors, based on prior experience and appeal.

Choosing a major—step #2: Read the course descriptions for the major, and imagine yourself studying the discipline for four years

After students narrow down their major to a few possibilities, I highly recommend that they *read the course descriptions for the major.* For instance, the Math major may contain advanced levels of conceptual math that are not needed if students are interested in business applications of mathematics. In this case, a strand of the Business major may be a more suitable option for one who possesses strengths in understanding mathematics, but wants to select a major where the discipline of math is applied in more practical ways, such as marketing. After reviewing the breadth of courses that are offered in the majors that undergraduates are considering, I urge students to imagine studying the proposed discipline for a minimum of four years. This is when students realize that they are ultimately the persons who will be affected by the final decision of the major. If an individual has grown up in a culture where there are expectations about pursuing a particular line of study or work toward a specific career, this is a critical time for the student to discuss his or her genuine interests with the family. It will not be your parents or other family members who will be waking up to attend classes, sit through the lessons, complete the homework, and take the exams. It will be *you.*

Choosing a major—step #3: Seek out resources on campus

On a university campus, it is to the student's advantage to consult these top three resources when selecting a major: (1) university students, (2) the Career Center, (3) an expert advisor. The combination of peer assistance and expert advice will help guide students to consider possibilities that were hitherto unknown, and affirm strengths and abilities geared toward a particular major.

Learn from your peers

It is valuable to hear the stories of other students—especially upperclassmen—when researching how to select a major. Their insider experiences may uncover pathways that may have never been thought of before. For instance, when I was an undergraduate, I had declared to be a Spanish major, but later, I met an upperclassman who had contracted an International Languages major and selected three languages (Spanish, French, and German) to study instead of just one language. Had I known that designing a customized course plan (a contract major) was an option, I may have explored that further. However, I had already invested too deeply in the Spanish major. Hearing others' stories exposes new college students to options and routes of study that were never conceived of before, and through enthusiastic peer testimonies, a path that was once closed or overlooked may be freshly opened.

Free resources at the career center

Most universities typically have a Career Center that offers multiple resources to support students in their academic and vocational journeys. I routinely schedule a visit to our Career Center with my first-year seminar students so that they can learn about its services, which include career inventories. I remember being directed to the Career Center when I was a first-year college student to complete the Myers-Briggs Type Inventory (MBTI). The questions on the assessment helped me to reflect upon my strengths, to confirm my interests in teaching, and to guide me toward the path of teaching. The services that the center offers are free to students, and the numerous resources available are extremely helpful.

Seek out a knowledgeable advisor

Before arriving at a college, most students are not familiar with all of the major programs, and do not know all of the possible routes to achieving their goals. Therefore, meeting with a college advisor who is familiar with the academic curriculum is helpful. In my own son's case, he had elected to be a Math major when applying to college because he was gifted with the math abilities that his mother was not. However, after speaking further with an advisor and reviewing the content of all the courses in the Math major, he decided that the Business major appealed to him more because he could still apply his math skills while being introduced to the world of marketing and economics. From his advisor, he also learned of the 4x1 major, where the university streamlined the BA + MBA programs so that Business majors could attain an MBA after adding just one more year to their undergraduate studies. This route allowed him to forego five business courses as well. This is an example of how students might have a particular interest, such as math, but are uncertain about the numerous programs and possibilities offered at the college that might match their future career goals more pointedly.

Today, I advise many of my freshmen in my first-year seminar course in this same way. I meet with each student individually to discuss their talents and interests and confirm the doors that can remain closed for them. I highlight obscure majors—such as Interpersonal Communications, Integrated Marketing, or others—that may not have been considered before in their decision-making. Additionally, if there is a student who admits not enjoying math or sciences, then I do not recommend any majors in those areas, while I will recommend such majors for those who are gifted in those areas. After selecting a few possible majors for consideration, the student then is encouraged to spend some time independently reviewing the course descriptions of the majors to see if one major appears more attractive than another. This step in selecting a major is critical because most college freshmen do not know about all of the major programs that exist before arriving at a university, so sitting down with someone who is knowledgeable about the different programs that the college offers is important. Sometimes, *this may not be your appointed advisor. This is okay.* I have advised many students who were not formally appointed as my advisees. They trusted me and knew that I was willing to help them. But in the end, it has always been the student who was proactive in scheduling the appointment and accepting my help. So, make the appointment if you need the guidance.

Consider the time commitment for the major

Another point to consider in a consultation with an advisor is how long it will take for the student to complete the requirements of a particular major. As an advisor, I always want to help craft a four-year plan that will maximize the number of college credits that the student entered college with and design a manageable load each semester or quarter for the student to handle, along with the consideration of studying abroad and extracurricular activities. Often, students can move the process along by taking summer courses or overloading on units, but registering for summer school usually does not avoid costs, and you do not want to take so many courses each semester that you do not enjoy the college experience. Fifteen units per semester is an average load; eighteen units are manageable, but challenging. The combination of classes that is taken will certainly impact one's overall load. If you travel abroad, there are particular classes, such as Humanities, that I always advise undergraduates to take while there. Studying internationally means taking the time to travel and enjoy being abroad. I do not recommend overloading on units during those semesters, especially if students are concerned with maintaining a specific grade point average.

What is a minor?

Another scenario that arises when students are selecting their courses is the notion of adding minors to their academic program. A minor is an area of study that generally involves an average of 20 units of coursework. The number of units varies upon the specific discipline. If a student is passionate about a certain area of study, it is plausible to acquire a minor. However, undergraduates should carefully consider the time investment that a minor will require, and they *should not be concerned with acquiring several minors as if they were awards.* Future employers will see these areas of concentration in applicants' resumes and interviews, so students should not simply take on the mentality that a minor is neither vital nor necessary. If it works out in conjunction with the major area of study and time frame, then one should consider it, but the other factors of time and tuition outweigh the simple title of adding a minor.

Double major or contracted major

If a student possesses interests in two specific areas of study and has the time to complete the course requirements for both majors, then a double major may be an option. Given that many students enter college with a number of credits due to Advanced Placement (AP) courses or online classes, it is more common to find room in their schedules to pursue a double major. Additionally, students may propose a contracted major, where courses from two or more disciplines could be combined to create a unique major. University professors and administration would need to approve the plan of study, but this is one approach to studying a multiple number of disciplines. Similar to the approach adopted when considering a minor, undergraduates should carefully calculate the time and tuition involved when considering a double major or a contracted major.

Life lesson: My personal story of selecting a major

When I entered college, I was a Biology major…for eight days. Ever since I was a child, I wanted to be a pediatrician. I had grown up in a home where both my Asian parents worked in the medical field—my father was a radiologist and my mother was a registered nurse. My parents took great pride that their daughter wanted to become a doctor. However, after arriving at college and scanning through all the documents that described the courses that I would have to take in my undergraduate career, I began to rethink my decision to become a doctor. The Biology major was heavy laden with chemistry courses, and I had avoided taking chemistry in high school because of my low self-confidence in my math abilities due to countless experiences with ineffective math teachers. Looking at the course content of the Biology major made me really think about how serious I was in committing myself to studying biology for my undergraduate career as well as moving on to medical school. Being physically separated from my family also made me think more carefully about what I wanted and not just what would please my family. The reality was that I was the one who would be attending all the classes and completing all the work. I knew that I would have to select a major that I would genuinely love—and so, I did.

There were moments during my college career when I had to independently and confidently make decisions and present them to my parents respectfully, and this was one of them. Sharing that my plans for my future were different from my parents' expectations was not easy, but it was necessary. In the end, they respected my decision not to pursue a career in medicine, even though I am certain that it was difficult for them. However, I believe that college is a time when you evolve independently as an adult, and choosing a major is one of the first opportunities to truly consider what you want for your future.

In my heart, I knew that I loved the idea of being a teacher. Growing up, I respected and admired my teachers and always enjoyed school. The first step I took was visiting the college Career Center to complete an inventory to see what types of careers matched my interests, even though I already knew that I wanted to be a teacher. (I could identify all the questions that most likely would lead to confirming my desire to be a teacher, so I may have skewed my own data.) Next, I met with a college professor who served as the advisor to the education program. She possessed the expertise to explain all the courses that were required to earn a teaching credential and reviewed my high school transcript with me so that she could help me compose the best four-year plan after considering the college credits I had already earned through AP courses. Although most students who want to be elementary school teachers selected Liberal Arts as their major, the advisor recommended a different plan for me. She noticed that I had passed the AP exam in Spanish and had taken an extensive number of Spanish classes in high school, so she suggested that I become a Spanish major. This strategy showed my future employers that I possessed an exceptional talent. To this day, I am so grateful to that advisor for her sage wisdom because demonstrating fluency in the Spanish language and having the credentials to back up my skills has proven to be extremely valuable in Southern California. I was also content that I had selected a major that was not only enjoyable, but also valuable. The lesson here is to consult with an expert advisor to help you uncover all your possibilities when deciding on a major. Before I entered college, I would have never dreamed of choosing Spanish as my major. It was only after meeting with an advisor, who helped me evaluate my strengths, consider my career goals, and review the majors with me, that was I able to feel confident about my choice for a college major.

Picking a Career Path: Ask "What are you interested in learning?" and not
"What do you want to do for the rest of your life?"

It is a daunting task for most university students—and even grown adults—to decide what professional pathway they want to commit to for the duration of their lives. Yet, people constantly ask college students: **What do you want to be? What do you want to do for the rest of your life?** I encourage students not to think of college as a time when they must decide upon one specific career, but as a training period where they are accumulating the knowledge, tools, and skill sets to help shape their professional identities. College is a time to discover one's passions and to begin uncovering professional interests, but one's career will undoubtedly change over a lifetime. Asking students what they want to do *for the rest of their lives* is unnecessary. More relevant questions are: **What are you interested in learning? Toward what fields do you see your talents being attracted?**

In our rapidly changing times, **many careers do not exist yet for today's college students.** In the field of educational technology alone, there are new positions and titles that were only recently launched. Formerly, an Instructional Technology Specialist, Learning Designer, and Virtual Reality Specialist were not common positions found in education, but now, many institutions are seeking talented employees to fill such roles. Therefore, picking a career path first, and then selecting a specific major to complete, is not the traditional route toward employment anymore. Instead, students should use the time spent in college to gather a plethora of tools that will equip them with a myriad of skills necessary for careers in the twenty-first-century job market.

Life lesson: Careers can change over time

In my freshman year of college, I identified that my interests were in teaching and believed that I was destined to be an elementary school teacher *for the rest of my life*. However, my career in education has undergone many changes over the years. Upon graduating from college, I was initially hired as a high school Spanish teacher, and I took the job so that I could get my foot in the door of a school district. In the subsequent year, I transferred to an elementary school, where I fulfilled my dream of being an elementary school teacher, and taught first grade. During that year, I realized that I missed all my high school students and the special relationships that

I had developed with them, so I ended up transferring back to the high school the following year. Ironically, I spent more years teaching high school than elementary school.

Eventually, I decided to pursue my graduate studies so that I could teach teachers, and now, I have spent the second decade of my career as a university professor. Although the knowledge, tools, and skill sets that I developed over the years prepared me for a career in education, *I was not pigeon-holed into one career for my entire life.* In college, I discovered my passion and interests in the field of education, and over time, there were many outlets for me to share my talents in this arena.

I did not have to decide and settle on one position for my entire life's career. This fact alone comforts many college students because the question of "What do you want to do or be for the rest of your life?" may not be a realistic one. During your undergraduate career, a guest speaker, a mentor, or a friend may uncover an area of study that you never realized existed. Along the path of your journey, you may also meet someone who reveals a prospect that you never imagined was possible. Be open to the opportunities. During your college years, explore opportunities, meet people, build a professional network, and equip yourself with a body of knowledge or a set of skills that will prepare you for when these moments arise.

Discover your vocation(s): What is the true purpose of your life?

It is time to ask yourself—is life as simple as just selecting a major, choosing a career, and living happily ever after? Could there be a deeper meaning to your life? At Pepperdine University, a faith-based institution, all freshmen are required to read an essay entitled "Finding Your Heart's True Calling" (https://community.pepperdine.edu/cfl/student-programs/reading-assignment/). Through this exercise, the author, Professor Gary Selby, urges incoming freshmen to consider how their college years could be viewed as a time to discover their "calling," or "vocation," and not just a time to acquire skills, so that they can be successful in this world. The author poses the question, "So when you begin to think about vocation, *the starting point is not your career but your ultimate purpose.* Regardless of what job you do for a living, what is your reason for being on the earth?" In their orientation materials, Pepperdine students are encouraged to consider these questions:

1. Who and what has God called you to become?
2. How can you discern that calling?
3. What would you identify as your greatest gifts and talents?
4. How can you use those gifts on behalf of other human beings, especially those who have little compared to those of us who have so very much?

The idea is that educated lives can be used for the greater good, and not simply to promote self-wealth and perpetuate social stratification. Whether students attend a faith-based institution or not, the idea of vocation is one in which students consider the deeper meaning and purpose of their lives, and in doing so, they contemplate the restoration and preservation of humanity through global perspectives and social justice.

I have witnessed numerous inspirational stories where college graduates dedicated their lives not only to their professions, but also for the greater good. For example, I have worked with several students who have studied education, law, or social justice, who went on to use their skill sets to support and maintain orphanages in Guatemala and Fiji, as well as educational programs in Rwanda. Additionally, there are medical doctors who spend their summers in the missionary fields of Third World countries or give financial aid to college students so that they may participate in summer undergraduate research programs to further their knowledge in the sciences. These testimonies demonstrate lives committed to a deeper calling, or a vocation.

In the book *Let Your Life Speak: Listening for the Voice of Vocation*, Palmer (2000) wrote, ***"Our deepest calling is to grow into our own authentic selfhood, whether or not it conforms to some image of who we ought to be.*** As we do so, we will not only find the joy that every human being seeks—we will also find our path of authentic service in the world. ***True vocation joins self and service"*** (p. 16). Students may not realize their vocation right away. Most of the freshmen in my first-year seminar courses have confessed that they did not know the definition for vocation, nor consider its role in their lives. Most freshmen are asked, "What do you want to be?" and not "What is your vocation?" The idea of vocation urges students to reflect upon how their lives will count for more than simply using their education and skills to fulfill the responsibilities of a career that rewards them monetarily with a comfortable life. The rudimentary question, "What do you want to be?" is taken to a deeper level and prompts students to consider how their journeys in college and beyond can lead to greater depths of self-fulfillment. Palmer (2000) described his understanding of vocation "not as a goal to be achieved but as a gift to be received. Discovering vocation does not mean scrambling toward some prize just beyond my reach but accepting the treasure of true self I already possess. Vocation does not come from a voice 'out there' calling me to become something I am not. It comes from a voice 'in here' calling me to be the person I was born to be" (p. 10).

TED Talk speaker Emilie Wapnick challenged young people to consider the possibility of possessing multiple vocations in her popular talk, entitled "Why Some of Us Don't Have One True Calling." In her speech, Wapnick (2015) introduced a new term called a "multipotentialite," and shared examples of successful individuals who are able to share their various talents in multidisciplinary formats. For example, Wapnick described the company Meshu, which was formed by the interests in "cartography, data visualization, travel, mathematics and design that created custom geographically inspired jewelry." The speaker proclaimed that innovation happens at the intersections of this diverse mixture of skills and experiences. Her inspiring TED Talk affirmed that individuals can celebrate and apply multiple talents through their vocations and not be limited to one traditional solitary path.

Discovering your vocation may be a novel concept, but it is one that prompts students to consider the deeper purpose and meaning of their lives. This introspective reflection is one that may begin in college and will continue throughout your life's journey.

Conclusion

College will pose many questions—from the moment that you apply. The key is to make informed decisions and to take advantage of all the resources that are at your disposal. Ask the faculty and staff who serve as experts at your institutions for advice, talk to your peers, and spend some time in meaningful self-reflection. The ultimate goal of college is not simply to graduate and start a career—this is too simple. College presents a journey that will help launch your discovery of who you are and what your legacy will be, both personally and professionally.

Reflective Summary

Discussion

1. What classes have you enjoyed taking in the past? Why?
2. What classes have you not enjoyed taking in the past? Why?
3. If you declared a major, why did you select that major?
4. Without researching the details of a specific career, what would be a dream job opportunity for you?

Application

1. Place the skills/qualities you possess as a student in the columns provided. Add others that you can think of that are not listed.

Qualities/Skills	Strengths	Weaknesses
Analyzing Contributing to discussions Math calculations Memory Networking Note-taking Oral Communication; presenting Reading Researching Seeking assistance Test-taking Time Management Writing		

2. Cross out all the departments listed below that you are NOT interested in pursuing further studies in as a college student.

Biology	Business Administration	Chemistry	Communications
Computer Science	Creative Writing	Economics	Education
English	Film Studies	French	German
Hispanic Studies	History	Integrated Marketing Communication	International Business
International Studies	Italian	Journalism	Liberal Arts
Mathematics	Media Production	Music	Nutritional Science
Philosophy	Physics	Political Science	Psychology
Public Relations	Religion	Sociology	Sports Administration
Sports Medicine	Theatre Arts	Theatre and Music	Theater and Media Production

3. Look up 3 majors at your college within the majors that you have left above that you did not consider for yourself. List what they are and what seems appealing or unpleasant about the courses for the major.
4. Share 3 careers that you have always considered or dreamed of doing.
5. How have you seen an example of a life that was used to better the world and not simply for personal gain?

CHAPTER 2

People

Understanding and Respecting Human Diversity

"You never really understand a person until you consider things from his point of view [...] until you climb into his skin and walk around in it."

— *Harper Lee,* To Kill A Mockingbird

When I initially decided to become a teacher, I was concerned that my career choice might be mundane. I often marveled at the teachers who boasted that they taught first grade or high school English for 40 years or more, and I wondered how these veteran teachers could routinely teach the same subject every year. I questioned if I could also do the same thing for so long. After I gained some experience as a classroom teacher, it became clear to me that teaching was not mundane at all. On the contrary, it was dynamic, unpredictable, and exhilarating. I asked myself what element from the world of education kept it from being monotonous and boring, and the answer was immediately obvious—it was the people.

People make life interesting, challenging, and fun. Human beings are complex creatures, and the interplay of widely assorted personalities creates an infinite number of distinct and meaningful experiences. *We all process, communicate, interact, and experience things differently, even when we dwell in the same environment*. This is why no two years in my educational career have been the same; people have continually made my experience in teaching uncommon and interesting. Over the years, my interactions with the multitudes of students and their families have also taught me that people are sensitive beings, and that poor word selection, an uneasy tone, or an unintentional misunderstanding can be hurtful and agonizing. Though beauty exists in the variance of our makeup, it also takes effort to understand our differences, to respect them, and to realize that misunderstandings are easy and that words matter. There is a valuable life lesson in communicating and getting along successfully with others, and this stems from respecting and understanding our diversity.

When students begin college, getting along with and appreciating others is a life lesson that presents itself right away. The college years launch a life of new beginnings, which includes a host of fresh faces and varied personalities. People are everywhere—from orientation, to classes, to clubs, jobs, dormitories and more. You will be surrounded by people. Understanding how you will manage new relationships, make time to rejuvenate yourself, set boundaries to succeed socially and academically, and avoid burning out in the college community—these are important life lessons that you will encounter. This chapter will share common frameworks for understanding people's personalities and uncovers methods to thrive in a socially rich environment.

The relationship hierarchy: Understanding varying levels of intimacy and interaction

Though there are various levels of intimacy in relationships, college students are catapulted into a heightened level of closeness immediately. Oddly, freshmen are not only expected to meet and study with a new community of strangers, but they are also expected to live with them. For this reason, it is important to understand the basic tendencies and backgrounds of people's personalities so that you can appreciate their space, behavior, beliefs, and actions in order for a harmonious living and learning environment to be attained.

I have personally construc-ted a hierarchy of relationships that outlines the varying levels of closeness when forming relationships, which begins with introductions and culminates in living together. At the founda-tional level, I believe that some people can make a good first impression and can represent a pleasant disposition for a

Living together

Traveling for a week or longer

Traveling on a weekend retreat

Spending the day together

Sharing a meal or coffee date

Meet & Greet

short period of time, like a meet and greet session. On the next level, it is enjoyable to share a meal or a longer amount of time with certain people with whom you might share common interests or whose company you enjoy. The higher levels of the relationship ladder represent closer levels of interaction, such as spending the day together, traveling for lengthy periods of time, or ultimately, living together. In these more intimate cases, many walls come down in people's personalities. *When the façade of superficiality disappears, people see the uncensored, raw emotions of others*. Given that students reach this high level of closeness in a university residen-tial setting, it is best to pause and understand the nuances of people's personalities. During the college experience, students will encounter every level of this relationship hierarchy as they are surrounded by a plethora of distinct personalities, both in and out of the classroom setting. Furthermore, the levels of closeness that students experience with others will not always follow a linear progression. It is possible—and not unlikely—that students will find themselves at the higher levels of the relationship hierarchy after a simple introduction. Navigating these unique relationships can be challenging without a proper understanding of human behavior.

Additionally, nonresidential students will still need to learn how to develop relationships with new people, and get along with diverse personalities exhibited by their peers and professors.

College opens a fresh chapter in life, where students do not attend school in the same comfortable setting that they are generally accustomed to with childhood friends or familiar faces from their TK-12 schooling experience. In order to invest in and become part of a community, nonresidential students may need to put more efforts forward to engage with people and make connections. This entails a proficient level of interpersonal skills.

Understanding human diversity using the essentials of MBTI & Colors

When students are separated from their families, live independently, and/or begin their college years, they will begin to gain a better sense of self and appreciate the origins from which they came. They will learn more about their own personalities, encounter new ones, and be challenged by the uniqueness of human diversity. There are many self-inventories available to help college students uncover details about their personality and work ethic. It is common for Career Centers at colleges and universities to offer assessments such as the MBTI (2014), StrengthsQuest (http://www.strengthsquest.com/home.aspx), Smalley's Animal Personality Test (https://www.smalley.cc/personality-quiz/), and Chapman's (1995) Love Language Inventory. Although they all offer interesting perspectives, I have found that two particular assessments are the easiest and most helpful for me to understand, teach, and recall. The following section will focus on the essential elements of two specific inventories that will assist you in understanding yourself and others better.

MBTI meets colors

There are numerous self-assessments available that help people get a better sense of themselves and their behavioral tendencies. The Myers-Briggs Task Inventory (MBTI) is one of the most prominently referenced personality assessments among college students and adults, and universities commonly encourage students to complete it. Based upon the psychological types that Carl B. Jung describes, the MBTI identifies four key elements of personality types:

1. Introversion (I)/Extroversion (E)—how individuals gain energy,
2. Sensing (S)/Intuition (N)—how they process information,
3. Thinking (T)/Feeling (F)—how people make decisions,
4. Judging (J)/Perceiving (P)—how humans assess situations and execute tasks.

A four-letter result, such as INFJ, is given to the applicant as a result of responding to a battery of questions, and there are a total of 16 personality prototypes available to help us understand our general behavioral tendencies.

There are also various renditions of personality tests connected with color. Among these assessments, the common premise is that a specific color defines a particular personality type. These colors may include, but are not limited to, gold, orange, white, blue, yellow, green, and red. So, a red personality type may denote the traits of a leader, or one who is driven, task-oriented, organized, and bold. After reviewing several versions of the color personality assessment (Ault & Barney,

2007), I have created a simplified framework to describe personality types using four basic colors: red, yellow, green, and blue. People may see that they have tendencies which exhibit a combination of two colors, such as red and yellow, but the general tendencies are most likely to be defined by one particular color. Below are the definitions of my customized color system:

Color	Symbol	Personality Type	Behavioral Tendencies	
Red	Fire	Leader	+	Driven, task-oriented, takes charge, list maker
			−	Impatient, insensitive
Yellow	Sunshine	Peacemaker	+	Wants everyone to be happy, helpful, optimistic, friendly, positive
			−	Indecisive
Green	Data; Spreadsheet	Rule Follower	+	Data-driven, organized, analytical; likes rubrics and guides, handbooks, or manuals
			−	Slow to move and initiate; not spontaneous; socially awkward; easily flustered when plans do not work; literal
Blue	Sky; Birds	People Person	+	Spontaneous, relaxed, goes with the flow; loyal; relationship builder, connector
			−	Procrastinates; overextends self; asks for exceptions

Both the MBTI and the Color Personality Outline offer interesting perspectives on human behavior and a framework for understanding diverse personalities. Given the numerous codes and vocabulary associated with the various personality inventories available, I have found it to be easy and helpful to whittle down the essentials of all the assessments into two vital bits of information gleaned from the aforementioned inventories: 1) Are you an introvert (I) or an extrovert (E)? In other words, from where do you get your energy? And, 2) with what color would you associate your personality, given the four-color framework that I have described?

MBTI: E or I is the essential element

By sharing a simple language to define personality types, people can identify and discuss human behavior using a common framework. Often, personality inventories apply terms that people do not regularly use and are difficult to recall. For example, I can remember that the first letter of the MBTI—E or I—stands for Extroversion or Introversion, but I always have to look up the rest of the acronyms. It is difficult for me to recall what N, F, or J stands for when explaining my personality type. I even thought it was peculiar that the letter "N" was used to represent "iNtuition," and words such as "feeling (F)" and "judging (J)" also needed further explanation because they did not share the universal negative connotation of being too sensitive or quick to judge. Personality inventories were invented not only to outline what the various personality types are, but also to give us a common vocabulary to discuss them. If the language is not easy to understand, then trying to understand and discuss our differences becomes even more difficult.

In terms of the MBTI, I find that what people remember the most is the *E (Extroversion) or I (Introversion)—from where people get their energy*. This element of one's personality has attracted more attention and research with the publication of Cain's (2012) book, *Quiet: The Power of Introverts in a World that Can't Stop Talking,* and in the author's TED Talk, entitled "The power of introverts." Cain's work dispels the common misconception that introverts are simply quiet, while extroverts are talkative. Understanding that introverts need time alone to recharge their energy and that being with people drains them and/or makes them anxious is an important lesson to learn, especially when living in a socially rich college environment where people are ubiquitous. If a college student declines an invitation for dinner or an activity, it might not be personal. Instead, the college student may just be an introvert who needs to have a quiet, solitary evening to regain the strength needed to face a new day filled with people. Extroverts, on the flip side, may seem depressed or tired if they are not engaged socially. In this case, an extroverted student may need to participate in a study group, work in a communal environment, or discuss a personal problem with a close friend in order to thrive. Thus, the notion of introversion vs. extroversion is not defined simply as the tendency of being quiet or talkative; rather, it is how human beings gain their energy.

While in college, it is helpful to pause and determine if you are an introvert or extrovert. Through this self-reflective activity, you will better understand your own needs for downtime or social stimulation and be able to pair yourself with partners and friends with whom you are most compatible, given these tendencies. Identifying your personal methods to attain energy will also help manage scheduling and relationships. *Introverts might need to purposefully schedule quiet times in their day, or balance out a day of the weekend packed with activity with one day of rest. Extroverts will benefit from socially rich weekends and active calendars*. By knowing if a roommate, friend, or significant other is an introvert or extrovert, one can respect that person's need to either go out and be with people or stay home for a quiet evening. Understanding how you or others around you gain their energy will help you thrive not only in college, but also throughout your life.

In personal and professional contexts, it is helpful to understand and respect the introverted or extroverted nature of those around you. In my personal case, I am an extrovert, whereas my husband is an introvert. He not only enjoys going on solitary hikes or backpacking trip, but he also needs to do this to refuel his social energy. On the contrary, being with people energizes me, so my husband respects that I need to go out with girlfriends or attend social events regularly. Together, we make efforts to find times where both of our personality types can be addressed and appreciated. In my professional life, it has also been beneficial to understand this aspect of my colleagues' personality types. For instance, when I travel with one of my introverted colleagues, I acknowledge that she needs some downtime alone after a long day of travel and being with people. She is happy to go out to dinner later, but she needs time to rest before doing so. Understanding the introverted or extroverted nature of my family, friends, and colleagues has helped me to respect their space and time, and in the end, I see how our relationships have benefitted greatly from this knowledge.

The universal language of describing personalities using four colors

One of my former students who had been working in the housing and residential life community once introduced me to a color system that described how basic colors are related to personality descriptions. After completing some research, I found a wide array of similar assessments using various colors. However, my students and I have found that it is easiest to recall the four basic colors and personality types presented in this chapter: *red, yellow, green, and blue*. These archetypes successfully cover people's general behavioral tendencies, and the *universal color codes have made it easy for individuals to remember their meanings*. For example, the color red is typically associated with fire, which depicts a strong, driven, task-oriented leader. *Yellow* denotes sunshine, which triggers happy thoughts of joy; yellow represents the friendly optimists who want to maintain peace and joy in communities. They are often known as the "people pleasers." Next, the color *green* symbolizes data (e.g., spreadsheets), which involve logic, calculations, and precision. Personalities associated with green are those who do not appreciate exaggerations; they want to know exact numbers if someone says, "A lot of people are saying…" How many is "a lot"? Green people are efficient; they like to follow rules and appreciate rubrics and guides. Lastly, the color *blue* symbolizes the sky and the birds. Blue personality types are free spirits who are deeply loyal and value relationships. They will get projects done, but spending time with people will take priority over any professional or academic task. They have a deep fear of missing out ("FOMO"), and they tend to ask for exceptions on their behalf.

After giving this basic explanation of the color code for personality types, students can recall and understand different behavioral tendencies right away. First, they recognize and acknowledge their own tendencies. Typically, they are quick to self-identify as they read through the descriptions, and they will wholeheartedly know which particular color represents their personalities. Next, students begin classifying their roommates, friends, or employers. One former student who classified herself as red confessed that she had a very difficult time living with a student who was blue. *The red student was organized, made her bed daily, and appreciated an immaculate room*. However, the *blue student was more free-spirited, did not make her bed regularly, and was comfortable throwing her clothes all over the dormitory while running in and out throughout the day*. If the blue student understood that the red student appreciated a little more order, she could have made efforts to keep her clothes in a certain area, rather than thrown about throughout the room. Additionally, *when two yellow people work together, it is difficult to get things done* because they do not want to hurt one another's feelings. So, if one person asks, "Which Powerpoint template do you like?" the other might respond, "Whatever you like!" After identifying personality types, compromises and challenges can be more quickly uncovered.

In my professional life, understanding colors has been helpful in the ways that I behave after recognizing other people's colors. For example, if I know that my colleague is green, then I avoid exaggerations and am very careful about using hyperboles. When referring to numbers of students involved in a certain incident, I am careful to recall an exact number, rather than generalizing a large number. In response to red colleagues, I typically reply to their emails more quickly than others. I know that it is difficult for them to wait for an answer, no matter the level of importance of the subject. I try to send them a quick message, if possible.

In this same way, I have shared the color code with my student teachers so that they can consider and respect the different personalities that they encounter while completing their student teaching. For instance, a student teacher is typically assigned to a mentor teacher, who they work with daily in their clinical experience. A University Field Supervisor also observes the student teacher. If a mentor teacher is red, and the student teacher is blue, this could lead to a contentious working relationship, and vice-versa. Similarly, if the red individual arrives at the school early and prepares to have everything in order ahead of time, while the blue individual enters the classroom right before the school bell rings to begin the day without having time to take out any materials for the day, this will raise conflict. Moreover, if a red supervisor emails a blue student teacher and receives no response for a couple of days, the supervisor could misinterpret this action as a sign of the student teacher not caring. I recommend that student teachers consider the personality types of those who they are interacting with to minimize conflict and prevent confusion. The color system has helped me and my students to speak the same language and to understand the behavioral tendencies of those around us. It helps us all not to take actions so personally, but to better understand that others function differently than we do. When we pause to consider a scenario from another perspective, it helps to avoid a misunderstanding or to extend some grace to someone who functions differently from ourselves.

Overcoming unconscious prejudice

One stark and usually sad tendency that I have learned and observed firsthand as an educational psychologist is that humans tend to gravitate toward those with whom they share the most similar characteristics. Why I use the adjective "sad" to describe this pattern in human behavior is because I believe that this can limit our learning potential and our experiences. For example, if teachers determined which students succeeded or failed simply based upon a student's physical appearance, then there would be no equal opportunity for people to succeed independently in schools. In this same way, this would limit the ability of certain students to reach their full potential, given the biased restrictions that the teacher would impose upon the students. Sadly, but realistically, *we are most comfortable with people who look like ourselves* and appreciate environments that replicate familiar reminders of our upbringings. *Unfamiliar people or surroundings make us feel uncomfortable.* This digresses from our "norm."

Whether we realize it or not, our minds have been primed to associate certain dispositions and qualities with particular races and appearances. In his book *Blink: The power of thinking without thinking*, Gladwell (2005) referred to the Implicit Association Test (IAT), and demonstrated to readers that different cultural contexts and environments have primed our unconscious minds to automatically form uninformed preconceptions about people and places. Gladwell (2017) claimed that the IAT measures one's level of "unconscious prejudice, that's the kind of prejudice that you have that you aren't aware of, that affects the kinds of impressions and conclusions that you reach automatically without thinking." After completing the IAT, 80 percent of Americans associated words such as "evil" and "failure" with black people, while pairing words such as "love" and "joy" with white people (Everyday Thomist, 2015). The media and other forces have implicitly conditioned our thoughts and behaviors.

In another excerpt of the text, Gladwell also called attention to the fact that over **58 percent of CEOs from Fortune 500 companies are tall men**. Even though only 14.5 percent of men in the United States are over 6 feet tall, more than half of the CEOs in these prominent companies possess this physical trait. In my observations of human behavior, I notice that height does affect how others behave. I am especially conscious of this conditioned response because I am only about 5 feet tall. After reading this valuable insight from *Blink*, I understood that I had many more challenges to overcome than someone who is tall.

I include these insights from Gladwell's text because it is important to acknowledge the unconscious priming of human behavior and to consciously combat it with intentional efforts to expose us to different people and environments. In this way, we can alter our unconscious prejudice and shape our minds in a positive way to embrace and learn from diversity, rather than shun it.

On the first day of my first-year seminar and my educational psychology courses, I have routinely taken on the character of a Korean immigrant professor with a thick Asian accent, and dressed up in an oversized dress suit, adorned with an obnoxiously colored paisley silk scarf, while wearing knee high nylons covered with white sports socks and chunky summer sandals. Using broken English throughout my speech and leaning into my students' personal space while we interacted, I carried on the act of being a funny, loud, and awkward Asian professor. During my lesson, I told my students that one of the most valuable "rife ressons" that they will learn is not to judge people before getting to know them because there is more to people than their outward appearance. Just as Lee (1960) wrote in *To Kill A Mockingbird*, *"if you can learn a simple trick, [Scout,] you'll get along a lot better with all kinds of folks. You never really understand a person until you consider things from his point of view [...] until you climb into his skin and walk around in it"* (p. 85). After making my students feel quite uncomfortable with my role play, I soon revealed that I was simply acting, and I shed my costume and my thick accent to reveal my true identity with my real wardrobe underneath my costume and my authentic American voice. Years later, students recount this valuable life lesson because it helps them to think about how they should consciously take a moment to alter their unconscious behavior before judging someone. In my educational psychology class, this lesson is particularly valuable for prospective teachers, who will encounter a diverse population of students from various backgrounds, talents, and cultures. College freshmen also find this lesson to be impactful as they meet a host of new people and learn how to thrive in new environments.

Conclusion: Understanding and embracing diversity

My hope is that as you begin college, and continue on in your life's journey, it will be helpful for you to understand the different behavioral tendencies of people, and you will embrace and not shy away from people who are different from yourself. I encourage you to take a moment to pause and recognize your unconscious biases, and to make intentional efforts to reach out to someone, even though your initial response might be not to do so. I have found that taking the conscious step to stop myself to pass quick judgment upon someone based on my conditioned response has reaped great benefits. People are different. We are all unique, and this great diversity should be welcomed and celebrated, rather than feared or avoided.

Reflective Summary

Discussion

1. Are you an introvert or an extrovert? Give personal examples to support your claim.
2. Based on the color personality outline, what color(s) best represent(s) you? Describe an incident that demonstrated this tendency.
3. Give an example of a person who demonstrated a color tendency that was frustrating to you. After identifying your own color, explain how you might have responded to their actions differently, or reached a better compromise.

Application

1. Fill out the tables below. Insert your answers in the first table, and then, ask 3 other people to respond to the same questions. Compare your answers and reflect upon why your answers may be similar or different.

Profession	Height	Gender	Race	Adjective
Elementary School Teacher				
College Professor				
Basketball Player				
Taxi Driver				
Computer Programmer				
Manicurist				

Profession	Height	Gender	Race	Adjective
Elementary School Teacher				
College Professor				
Basketball Player				
Taxi Driver				
Computer Programmer				
Manicurist				

Profession	Height	Gender	Race	Adjective
Elementary School Teacher				
College Professor				
Basketball Player				
Taxi Driver				
Computer Programmer				
Manicurist				

Profession	Height	Gender	Race	Adjective
Elementary School Teacher				
College Professor				
Basketball Player				
Taxi Driver				
Computer Programmer				
Manicurist				

2. Draw lines from one column to the other. Each word can only be used once. There are no correct answers. This is a simply an exercise to see how you connect the words. Go with your immediate instincts.

Column A	Column B
Mother	Tall
Father	Family
Actress	Work
Executive	Math
Athlete	Blonde
Asian	Rich

3. Read the statements below. Compose a response to each statement, given the different color personality type that follows each quote.
    a. "All of my friends are rushing a sorority/fraternity, but I'm just not sure that I can afford it. I have no money." [How would a GREEN personality type respond?]
    b. "It is clear that my professor just doesn't care about the students because I haven't heard from him in two days about my request for a letter of recommendation." [How would a YELLOW personality type respond?]
    c. "I know that I need to pick up my room and study but I need to spend some time with my friend from class who is having a rough day." [How would a RED personality type respond?]

CHAPTER 3

Communication

Written and Oral Expressions as a College Student

> "The single biggest problem in communication is the illusion
> that it has taken place."
>
> — *George Bernard Shaw*

Words. Perspective. Timing. Intention. Context. Audience. Style. These are just a few of the critical elements that people must consider in order to communicate effectively. One unique feature about human beings is our ability to communicate with one another through written and oral expression. The college years will increase the number of contexts in which students will have to interact with others. On campus, students might talk or send emails to administrators, faculty, staff, teacher assistants (TAs), residential advisors (RAs), roommates, classmates, and friends. Additionally, students will continue to communicate with people off campus, such as employers, parents, friends, and family. These diverse professional and personal contexts will cause students to consider the various aforementioned factors that will affect the tone and deliverance of their message. Mastering the art of communication is a life lesson that will prove to be vital, both in and out of the classroom. This chapter presents helpful tips to consider when communicating with others in both written and oral forms.

Written communication

In today's digital age, people write exponentially more due to our ubiquitous access to digital tools. *USA Today* reported, "More people are writing more frequently and in more formats. There are more than 2 billion email users; 180 million blogs; 400 million daily tweets; and 8.6 trillion SMS annual text messages" (Budig & Heaps, 2013). The surge in social media has opened even more opportunities for the written word to be shared publicly. Our ability to post our thoughts immediately online for the public to read has become both a blessing and a curse. Without the proper consideration of vital elements such as timing, word choice, style, and tone, one's written message can be grossly misinterpreted or regretfully published. On the contrary, with careful attention to the composition of one's written message, opportunities can be opened, and relationships can be strengthened. For these reasons, it is imperative that students consider the implications of their written words as they enter their college years and begin their professional lives.

Three main areas in which students will experience using the written word regularly to communicate in college and beyond are: (1) emails, (2) essays or reports, and (3) personal correspondences, such as Thank You cards. First, students will compose written messages daily in their digital communications with peers and adults. It is critical that students learn how to discern personal and professional contexts for their email exchanges and to compose messages accordingly. Next, students will find their scholarly voice as they use the written word to carry out their academic responsibilities. It is important for students to avoid colloquial expressions and to develop their formal writing skills. Lastly, I encourage college students to exercise the written word in personal correspondences. Though handwritten cards appear to be a lost art in today's digital age, they are still greatly valued and appreciated. Within these contexts, students will find it valuable to carefully practice the art of communicating using the written word.

Written Communication: How to Compose a Professional Email

After enrolling in a university, students are automatically given their own email address with the school's name attached to it as part of the registration process. Upon receiving this gift, there is an expectation to log in daily and interact with others routinely via this written mode of communication. Although studies have indicated a decline in college students' engagement with emails, this method of communication is still pervasively used to connect with professors or other professional people in the business world (Radicati, 2014; Straumsheim, 2016). Using the email system, students can easily access the contacts from their college network, and thereby, reach out not only to their peers, but also to administrators, faculty, and staff. Students must be mindful of their audience so that the appropriate tone, voice, and length can be presented in the written message. This may be particularly difficult for students who have not received any guidance or instruction on how to compose any type of written message to a professional person, such as a faculty member or university administrator.

How to address a college professor

One of the first lessons that I teach my first-year students is how to address professors in college. Most students who are beginning their initial year in college have just graduated from high school, where it is common to refer to teachers as "Mr." or "Mrs./Ms./Miss." However, in higher education, a different academic culture exists because professors have acquired doctoral degrees, accompanied with the title "Ph.D. or Ed.D." Thus, it is customary to address professors by their professional title of "Dr." If students are not certain if a professor has completed a doctoral degree, then it is recommended that students use the title of "Professor" to address the instructor. It is better to err on being too formal, rather than too casual. *[*Use Dr. or Professor to address university faculty.]*

How to format a professional email

Additionally, starting college will propel students into the world of professional emails. In higher education and beyond, there will be daily occasions when emails will be sent and exchanged with people on whom you will want to leave a positive and respectful impression and from whom you will want to receive an encouraging or inviting response. Therefore, it is necessary to thoughtfully compose an email message. A greeting, line spacing, word choice, and a salutation are all critical elements that work together to convey tone in an email.

Below are two examples of typical emails that could be sent to a college professor. The initial email does not consider formatting, tone, or word choice, while the latter does. It is important to note the differences between the two emails and the different messages that are conveyed, even though their objectives are the same.

Email Example #1: Professional Email Fail

Hey, Mrs. Erbes!!

   I'm in your education class this semester. I don't understand why I got such a bad grade on my research paper!!! I have never spent so much time on a paper IN MY LIFE, and I don't think I deserve this grade. This really doesn't seem fair. I think that you should read the paper again. When can I come by this week to talk to you about this??

John

Email Example #2: Professional Email Example

Hello, Dr. Erbes.

   My name is John Doe, and I am a student in your education class that meets on Mondays and Thursdays from 10–12 this semester. I am writing to see if you have any time available this week for an office appointment. I would like to discuss the research paper that you recently passed back in class.

   I invested quite a bit of time on this paper and was disappointed with my final grade. I would like to learn how I could improve my writing in the future. I would appreciate any guidance that you could offer.

   I look forward to meeting with you.

Best,

John

In the first email, the writer begins with a very informal greeting. I recommend that students ***never begin their emails to professional people with "Hey."*** This is a colloquial term and should not be used to greet a professor. Additionally, the student uses the personal title of "Mrs." when a more respectful address should implement the professional title of "Dr.," "Professor," or even "Dean." Following the opening line, there is no white space to separate the different parts of the message. Instead, the content appears as one block of text, without any space for the eyes to break up the different elements of the email. *[*Break up an email with line spacing.]* Although it is clear that the student is angry about the grade that was earned on the research paper, his poor choice of words immediately puts the reader on the defensive. The message also conveys an immature and disrespectful tone and ends abruptly without a salutation. Given that the written word is tangible, and can be copied or forwarded to other parties, it is critical to be mindful of not writing anything that will be regretted later. Time is another essential factor to consider when communicating with others. It is highly recommended not to compose an email while emotions are charged with anger, and to have someone else proofread an important email to get a second opinion before sending it. *[*Don't compose an email when angry.]* Often, I compose an email in the evening, save it to my drafts folder, and then return to it in the morning to read it again. Allowing some time to pass gives me the opportunity to step away from the situation, and then, return to it with fresh eyes. This may shed some new light or perspective on the incident that was not considered before in the heat of the moment. Additionally, I usually *consider the time of day when I send important emails*. I am mindful that my recipients may not give work email their full attention if my message is sent after business hours—which typically is after 5 p.m. and before 8 a.m.—and weekends. Disregarding key elements, such as tone and timing, when composing and sending a professional message, will make the subsequent personal encounter with the recipient even more difficult.

The second email effectively uses word choice and line spacing to convey a professional and respectful tone. The greeting begins with the recipient's professional title, and is followed appropriately with a line space to help break up the different components of the message. The student also specifies the course section he is enrolled in, which is especially helpful if there is more than one section of the class that is offered. Instead of putting the professor on the defensive, the composer of the second email respectfully shares his disappointment in the research paper grade and also uses the proposed meeting as an opportunity for learning. During the office appointment, the student can then learn: a) what the perspective of the professor was when assigning the grade, and b) how his writing can be improved in the future. The email ends with an appropriate salutation, which concludes a respectful, well-crafted message. A proper greeting, adequate line spacing within the content, formal diction, and a fitting salutation comprise the vital elements of a professional email.

Use a list format to highlight main points

It is also helpful to break up email messages that include an excessive amount of information to guide the reader through dense content. Our minds have become classically conditioned to read materials such as web pages, searching for hyperlinks or headings that highlight the most pertinent information. Formatting a message that contains a lot of information in this way will infuse scaffolds that draw attention to the main points of the text. The following message demonstrates how dividing the content of an email using a list or bulleted format assists the reader in deciphering the important information.

Email Example #1: Dense Content

Dear Dr. Erbes,

Hello. I am a freshman in your first-year seminar class that meets on Mondays and Thursdays this semester from 8 a.m. to 10 a.m. I am preparing my four-year plan and have some questions. I am hoping that you can help me. I took the AP test in history, but it looks like I still have to take a history class. Is this common? Also, I would like to study abroad, but I'm not sure if I will be able to graduate in four years if I do this. And, is there any scholarship money available through the department that can help me with taking an extra summer class if needed?

Thank you for your help,

Maria

Email Example #1: Break Up Dense Content with a List

Dear Dr. Erbes,

Hello. I am a freshman in your first-year seminar class that meets on Mondays and Thursdays this semester from 8 a.m. to 10 a.m. I am preparing my four-year plan and have some questions:

1. **AP CREDIT:** I took the AP test in history, but it looks like I still have to take a history class. Is this common?
2. **STUDYING ABROAD:** I would like to study abroad, but I'm not sure if I will be able to graduate in four years if I do this. Do students usually stay longer if they study abroad?
3. **SCHOLARSHIP**: Is there any scholarship money available through the department that can help me with taking an extra summer class if needed?

Thank you for your help,

Maria

The life lesson that is presented in these examples is the art of communicating with others via email. Students need to be mindful of the following critical elements when composing a message: (1) appropriate greeting and title of recipient, (2) line spacing and bulleted formats to break up the dense content of an email, (3) careful word choice, tone, and timing, and

(4) respectful salutation. Integrating these various components when crafting a professional email will serve students well in college and beyond.

Written Communication: How to Develop an Academic Voice

In addition to emails, college students will develop their writing skills while completing class assignments, essays, or research papers. There is a formal vernacular that is adopted when engaging in a scholarly community, and students must learn the nuances of this academic culture. *Formal reports will not use the same language as personal emails.* Understanding the audience, and adapting one's writing appropriately, is essential. Learning, and adopting the proper language of a particular community, is customary when being introduced to any new culture. This proves true not only with ethnic groups, but also in other community situations, such as when surfing, dancing, playing music, and even when ordering drinks in coffee shops. One must learn the language of the respective culture in order to communicate with the other surfers about the ideal water conditions, to perform particular dance movements, to play specific rhythms in a song, or to order their favorite espresso drink. In this same way, participating in an academic or professional community encourages young adults to be mindful of diction, audience, and writing style in order communicate eloquently using professional language.

Developing Professional Writing through Diction

Diction—or *word choice—is a key element when elevating one's writing*. A simple step in developing academic writing is to select words that are not ordinary and conversational. Instead, the writer can incorporate more vivid and advanced vocabulary to illustrate the main points. This can easily be done with the aid of a thesaurus, if needed. Students should review their writing and select common words that can be transformed. It is also helpful to avoid using contractions, such as "can't" or "don't," to create a more formal tone. Below are examples of how average sentences can be transformed easily with diction.

Examples of Ordinary Sentences Transformed with Proper Diction

Ordinary Sentence	Transformed Sentence
The student *got* an A in math even though he *couldn't figure out* the homework problems.	The student *earned* an A in math even though he *had difficulty solving* the homework problems.
I didn't have *enough time* to *look up more* than four articles.	Due to the *limited time* given to complete this assignment, this report *references* only four articles.
Our hypothesis *is* that there *will be no more* liquid in the beaker.	Our hypothesis *proposes* that the liquid in the beaker *will dissolve.*
The teacher was so *bad* that everyone *failed* the class.	Given the *ineffective* teaching methods of the professor, it was *difficult for students to pass* the class.
The author *said* that cell phones *aren't good* for kids because they *don't help* their attention span.	The author *concluded* that cell phones *negatively impact* the attention spans of young people.

Formal writing should prompt students to *consider their audience*. A research paper, or a professional email, should not take on the same casual tone as a conversation with a friend. A college professor, or an academic audience, will seek the appropriate application of diction, line spacing, smooth transitions, and clear organization. Being mindful of these elements when constructing formal writing will serve students well in their college years and beyond.

Written Communication: Expressing Gratefulness through Thank You Cards

College students have numerous opportunities to practice writing Thank You notes. However, if they have not been encouraged or taught how to do this while growing up, then students may not understand how to compose such a note or realize its great value. For this reason, the following section will shed light on the value of handwritten Thank You notes and present a template for a simple note of gratitude.

In my college courses, I encourage students to send Thank You messages to university faculty, staff, or others whenever possible. People appreciate knowing that their time and efforts were helpful, and following up a generous act of kindness with a Thank You note is one way that students can express their gratefulness. An electronic message has become the default method to express thanks in our digital society. Although it is convenient to send a quick note of thanks using text or email, a handwritten Thank You card is an inexpensive gift that is greatly appreciated and underused. Purchasing a set of Thank You cards is a worthy investment for college students, and it is easy to locate decorative cards in the dollar section of numerous stores. Given that freshmen are new members to the college community, it is likely that they will receive special assistance in some way as they navigate their initial year in college. The exercise of writing Thank You cards is an art that we should all practice to develop grateful attitudes and express sincere appreciation for those who assist us along the path of our life's journey.

One might assume that it is customary for students to *write handwritten Thank You notes*, but sources such as the *Harvard Business Review* (2013) and the *Wall Street Journal* (2012) confirmed that it is indeed rare. This was validated in my own experiences at my small university. As a method to build community, professors at my institution are encouraged to host students in our home for dinner. In my 15 years at the university, I have extended this dinner invitation to all my classes almost every semester. Students consistently enjoy the event, and have shared their gratitude verbally or occasionally through email. I have received handwritten Thank You notes from less than 1 percent of the students over the years. Each time I have received a card from the students, it has been a special gift and very memorable. This simple example brought attention to the fact that handwritten notes are uncommon.

The format of a note of gratitude does not need to take on a long or complex structure. Like the suggestions shared when crafting a professional email, the writer of a Thank You note should: (1) begin with a respectful greeting, (2) briefly describe the specifics of the recipient's noteworthy act and express appreciation, and (3) conclude with a salutation. Here is an example for a simple Thank You note:

Thank You Note Example

Dear Dr. Erbes,

Thank you for taking the time to write a letter of recommendation for me.

I know that you are very busy, and I sincerely appreciate the time you spent on my behalf. I value for your support and will keep you posted on the next steps of my process.

Gratefully,

John Doe

In this same way, I encourage my students to *send Thank You notes to potential employers after being interviewed.* These employers may be on or off campus. For example, when students interview for an internship, a study abroad program, or a work-study position in a university office, I recommend that they always follow up with a Thank You note. Trebay (2014) confirmed that the act of writing a Thank You card not only sets you apart from the majority of the people being considered for such position, but it also begins to shape your personality and reputation as a respectful, grateful, and polished individual. Writing a Thank You note on behalf of a group also propagates the poised and professional image of that entity as well.

I truly believe that it is not simply the tangible gift of the handwritten Thank You note that authenticates this important life lesson of gratitude. Moreover, it is the expression of the many fine qualities of the writer that the recipient recognizes from this kind act. Thank You notes exhibit the writer's grateful heart, attention to detail, and thoughtfulness. When requesting a letter of recommendation or being considered for a position of employment, these are the exceptional qualities that will set individuals apart from the ordinary population.

Oral communications: Professional and personal contexts

College students will encounter numerous occasions when they will have to express themselves verbally to peers and adults. Sharing compliments, or affirming someone, is easier than selecting the appropriate words to confront another person about matters such as living style, study habits, a grade dispute, or a program decision. The following section offers suggestions on how to discuss various topics in such professional and personal contexts.

Confrontations: It's not About "You"

Navigating confrontations can be uncomfortable and difficult when not handled carefully. In college, various situations will arise with roommates (or professors) when students might feel compelled to express their feelings. The choice of words used, as well as the approach selected to broach a sensitive subject, profoundly impacts how a message is received. It is recommended that the speaker *avoids accusatory "you" statements,* encases the criticism or point of distress with some positive comments, and is mindful of the recipient's method of processing information.

First, in a confrontational situation, it is best to begin with asking, "How does this matter make me feel?" and not to focus solely on the actions of the other parties involved. In this way, you can begin expressing your personal feelings and not initiating with statements that direct blame or assign fault upon others. In the table below, there are comparative statements that demonstrate how the tone of a discussion can be shaped more positively by the way one's sentiments are personally expressed:

Examples of Comparative "You" and "I" Statements

"You" Statements	"I" statements
Your clothes are never put away, and you never clean up your stuff. Our room is a mess because of you!	Our dorm room is a small space, and it is difficult for me to live in a tight area that's not picked up. I would really appreciate it if you could tidy your side more, and keep things cleaner.
You never told us that you wanted the research formatted in any particular way or how many sources you wanted us to use. I could have gotten an A on my paper if I had known this.	It was frustrating for me to realize that there was a specific way to format the research paper and an expectation for a minimum number of sources. It would have been helpful if this were communicated before the paper was completed. This made a significant difference in my grade, and I would like to discuss the possibility of raising my grade by making revisions or completing an additional assignment.
You only picked people for the study abroad program who were involved with Greek life. You clearly have a bias toward a particular student group. How can others ever be given a fair chance?	After reviewing who was accepted into the study abroad program, I found it peculiar that all those who were admitted were involved in Greek life. Could you help me understand the selection process better?

It is clear that starting a discussion with "you" statements sets a negative and angry tone. By expressing one's personal feelings first, and then, following up with a description of the matter at hand, the discussion is set up for a constructive dialogue. Avoiding words that will trigger stress before or during the meeting is also beneficial when trying to establish the proper tone for a discussion. Phrases such as "We need to talk" or "You never _____" make people feel defensive, so it is helpful to choose one's words carefully, or the discussion may begin with heightened levels of tension before it has even begun.

Cookie the Comment

Additionally, when sharing one's feelings with another person, it is useful to "cookie" the comment, or to sandwich a concern between two affirmations. This strategy creates a more pleasant interaction and expresses compassion and sensitivity during a confrontation. The following table presents examples of this approach:

Example of Modifying a Direct Statement: Cookie the Comment

Direct Statements	Cookie the Comments
(to a roommate) I really need you to pick up your things. Our room is a mess because of you!	1. (+) I have enjoyed getting to know you this semester as my roommate. 2. Since our room is so small, I would really appreciate it if you could pick up your things a bit more or keep them in your area. 3. (+) I think that this would really help both of us keep track of our things better.
(to an employer) You scheduled me to work this week during the times that I told you that I needed off to study. I cannot work these hours!	1. (+) I love this job and am happy to work whenever I am able to do so. 2. However, I had submitted a reminder to let you all know that I will not be able to work some particular hours this week due to midterms. 3. (+) I would really appreciate it if you could revise my schedule, and I'm open to making up hours on a different week, if that is needed.

Using this approach to encase a concern between two positive statements is a strategy that sets a pleasant and constructive tone to a serious discussion.

Processing Time

We all process information differently, and some people need more time to unpack information and compose a verbal response. In her book *Quiet*, Cain (2012) disclosed that **introverts process information internally and are not as quick to respond as extroverts.** Knowing this, it is helpful to discover if others need time to process, or prepare mentally, before meeting to verbally express their thoughts about particular matters. In these cases, it is beneficial to schedule meetings at specific times, and to share an agenda or list of questions that will be covered during the encounter. This brings comfort and ease to certain individuals because they will have ample time to prepare their thoughts, rather than being expected to rapidly respond to others on the spot. Another benefit of this strategy is that it gives people time to reflect carefully on a given situation, rather than lashing out in an emotionally charged moment—which often leads to regretful remarks. At first, scheduling pointed conversations was an unusual concept for me to comprehend because I am an extrovert, and additionally, as a teacher, I have always had to respond without hesitation. However, my husband is an introvert and processes information differently than I do. When discussing matters related to our children, finances, or our relationship, I have seen how giving my husband time to prepare for our discussion decreases stress and increases constructive interactions during our meetings. Although it may seem odd initially, determining a time to chat about a particular topic may actually allow both parties to prepare more effectively for a fruitful discussion.

Communicating with school and family

Our digital culture has made written communications via email, text, and social media posts more common than talking on the phone or meeting with people in person. Although texting is the preferred method for college-aged youth to communicate (Skierkowski & Wood, 2012), talking on the phone or meeting someone face-to-face is not completely obsolete. Professional and personal relationships are built on social exchanges, and navigating the paths of written versus oral communication can be a challenge for new college students. It may be intimidating for freshmen to speak to adults or upper classmen at the university; however, this should not deter students from engaging in these personal interactions. Additionally, students will discover the challenge that lies in fostering relationships with family and friends back at home while being away at college. Although it is convenient and easy to send a quick text or email, a personal call—or hearing someone's voice—is a personal and treasured gift that should not be taken for granted. The written approach may appear more passive than the active approach of talking to someone, and with maturation, college students will learn how to balance these methods of communication in the contexts of school and home.

Communicating at School: Talk to your Instructors

In small or large universities, it is beneficial for students to personally interact with professors or teaching assistants (TAs). **Attending office hours** are an ideal time to actively engage with instructors. In some contexts, it is acceptable to reach out to faculty to schedule a personal appointment, lunch, or coffee date. At my university, the Office of Student Affairs encourages faculty to dine in the cafeteria with students, so the school offsets the costs of the meals with a dining card. This is a strategy to help support community-building at the institution. The university system is different than pre-collegiate institutions, where students may have spoken more regularly on a daily basis with their instructors. At the college level, it is easy to be a passive student, independently learning, and choosing to attend classes or not. However, it is beneficial for college students to meet one-on-one with expert faculty who will advise them to better understand course content (or class scheduling) if the university culture supports such interactions. When grade disputes, or other matters, such as a need for a letter of recommendation arise, the instructor will recognize the student and be able to draw upon their personal interactions. Though it can be intimidating to meet with university instructors, students might find it easier to express themselves verbally and to receive immediate responses to their concerns in a personal appointment. Talking to faculty outside of class is encouraged and will prove to be helpful in one's college journey.

Communicating with Home: Talk to your Family

Communicating with family back at home can be challenging as a college student. Some students excel at talking to their parents (or loved ones) regularly, while others find it difficult to carve out the time in their impacted college schedule to personally reach out to those from home. The key is to **be intentional about talking to family and friends regularly from home.** For freshmen, or those who have moved away from home for the first time, the idea that one should purposefully connect with family is a new concept. Earlier, students would see their family daily, but now this dynamic has changed. Students will now participate in a community and begin a life that is separate from family. It is important to be cognizant of this change and to make intentional efforts to share your new life with family through personal interactions, whenever possible. Parents genuinely appreciate a personal conversation, rather than relying solely on social media posts that share your college happenings. With video conferencing options available, such as FaceTime, Skype, and Google Hangouts, the ability to talk remotely while simultaneously seeing each other's faces makes the interaction even more personal and easily accessible. Learning how to maintain personal communications with family is an important life lesson that students will encounter early on in their college years and will continue to manage throughout their lives.

Conclusion

Our voice. Our words. Our texts. Our emails. Our essays. All of these elements comprise our human interactions. Learning how to communicate with others is a complex process that involves understanding the dynamics of audience, culture, tone, timing, diction, and intention. Words can fortify relationships and promote opportunities or hurt people and limit prospects. Students will begin to shape their identities and find their own voices as they learn to communicate with others as an independent adult. The words that students choose to represent their written and oral expressions will serve as extensions of their minds and hearts. It is valuable for students to wisely consider how they should cultivate the art of communicating with others.

Reflective Summary

Discussion

1. Describe an incident when you needed to confront a faculty member or peer about something. What tip did you gain from this chapter that affirmed your action or caused you to think of how you could have handled the situation differently?
2. When is the last occasion you wrote a Thank You note? Describe the nature and format of the letter.
3. Describe a time when someone shared a concern with you. Why does this particular incident stand out to you? How was the information conveyed to you? How did you receive it?
4. What method of communication do you prefer more: verbal or written? Phone calls or texts/emails? Explain why.

Applications

1. What are five different greetings you could use to begin an email?
2. What are five different salutations that you could use to conclude a Thank You card?
3. Reword the following sentence, applying a respectful tone:
   (to a professor): "You changed the date for our next quiz, and I have no idea when it is."
4. Reword the following sentence using the "cookie the comment" approach (to a roommate): "I can't go to sleep because you keep the light on and stay up so late after I go to bed."
5. What are three different ways that you could reword the following two statements?

I really don't like when you . . .	1.
	2.
	3.
I can't do this. I just don't get it.	1.
	2.
	3.

CHAPTER 4

Time Management

How to Manage Time Efficiently in College

"This is the key to time management –
to see the value of every moment."

— *Menachem Mendel Schneerson*

One of the key life lessons learned in college is how to manage time efficiently. This is the greatest challenge that the majority of college students struggle with in these transformational years. When students do not utilize their time wisely, the disappointing outcomes include, but are not limited to, low class performance, illness, broken relationships, unfulfilled self-expectations, and anxiety attacks. On the contrary, when students use their time constructively, they are content, productive, and are thriving members of the university community. This chapter introduces the unique schedule of college classes, explains the challenges in balancing sleep, study, and social life, and presents useful strategies that help college students organize and optimize their time.

A new class schedule with freedom and flexibility

The open class schedule is one of the first elements of university life that is most novel or surprising to students who transition from high school to college. After attending class daily from 8 a.m. (or earlier in some cases) to 3 p.m. during their pre-collegiate years, it is initially odd (and delightfully exciting) for college students when they discover that their courses do not meet every day. It is typical for the common 4-unit class to be offered twice a week for two hours at a time, such as Monday and Wednesday from 2–4 p.m. Other 4-unit classes may meet four days a week for an hour each time, or for one block of four consecutive hours. The diverse selection of times for course offerings allows students to piece together a unique schedule that gives them more daily freedom and flexibility—a concept that was most likely absent from their traditional high school schedule. Those who were homeschooled, or participated in online schooling, may be more familiar with this type of scheduling, and may understand better the discipline necessary to succeed in such a fluid environment.

In college, students can choose when they would like to take their classes. So, if morning sessions, especially at 8 a.m., are unattractive to someone who is not an early riser, then the option of selecting classes that meet later in the day is available. Courses are also offered in the evenings; thus, it is possible to attend class during 6–8 p.m. or even 6–10 p.m. It is also feasible to arrange one's coursework in such a way that a whole day could be left open without any classes scheduled. Many college students try to protect a Friday or Monday so that they can take advantage of a 3-day weekend. Moreover, undergraduates typically enroll in only 4–5 classes, which is less than the normal course load assumed in high school. As a result, once a student's class schedule is completed, it appears less impacted than what they may have been accustomed to before college. What was once a tightly packed puzzle is now seen as an open frame with many floating pieces. ***This open schedule looks easy and appealing for new college students, but herein lays the trap.***

High School Schedule

Monday	Tuesday	Wednesday	Thursday	Friday
Classes: 8 a.m.–3 p.m.				
Extracurricular activities + Homework: 3 p.m.–11 p.m.				

College Schedule with Average Load of 15 Semester Units

	Monday	Tuesday	Wednesday	Thursday	Friday
8–9 a.m.					
9–10 a.m.		SPAN 101	SPAN 101	SPAN 101	SPAN 101
10–11 a.m.	ENG 101			ENG 101	
11 a.m. –12 p.m.	(10–11:30)			(10–11:30)	
12–1 p.m.					
1–2 p.m.	MATH 102	MATH 102	MATH 102	MATH 102	
2–3 p.m.	HUM 111			HUM 111	
3–4 p.m.	(2–3:30)			(2–3:30)	
4–5 p.m.		ART 101			
5–6 p.m.					
6–7 p.m.					
7–8 p.m.					
8–9.p.m.					
9–10 p.m.					
10 p.m. +					

Sleep, study, and social life

The open blocks of time in a college student's schedule will quickly be filled with homework, research, a job, social events, and other activities. If students utilize time intentionally, then they feel purposefully-driven, enriched, and accomplished. But when students do not use the time responsibly, they feel unorganized, burned out, and stressed. During various college orientations, I have commonly heard university representatives state that there are three main components of college life: *(1) sleep, (2) studies, and (3) social life. When time is not managed properly, one of these elements will always suffer.*

Protect Adequate Sleep Time

One of the first common challenges that I observe college students facing is establishing a healthy sleep pattern. Living in a building with numerous other young adults, and not having family present to set boundaries and monitor activities, leads to the temptation of staying up late, socializing with others. If time during the day was not spent constructively, then college students use the late evenings to catch up on their studies. It is not uncommon for me to see assignments uploaded at 2 a.m., to view emails sent at 4 a.m., or to hear of students staying up all night—what college students refer to as "pulling an all-nighter." These unhealthy sleep patterns have become part of the rites of passage of a college student. In her article, "*Is sleep deprivation the new college norm?*" Baltz (2016) confirmed, "There is so much happening on college campuses, both academically and socially, that sleep and rest are very low on most students' lists of priorities. As a freshman, I just thought that sleep deprivation was simply one of the aspects of college culture that I would be forced to adjust to." Because students have difficulty managing their time effectively, sleep schedules are one of the first areas of students' lives that are negatively impacted.

When human beings do not acquire enough sleep, they do not function properly. Hershner and Chervin (2014, p. 74) defined sleep deprivation "as obtaining inadequate sleep to support adequate daytime alertness." The researchers confirm that *more than 70 percent of college students attain insufficient sleep*. After reviewing literature that addressed the prevalence of sleep deprivation among college students, the researchers validated that *inadequate sleep negatively impacts students' memory, learning potential, academic performance, driving, and mood*. These findings were also substantiated in my personal observations of college student behavior. When I speak to parents during freshman orientation, I warn them that their students will most likely become sick in about one month. At that point, students' bodies usually wear down from lack of sleep and overstimulation. Their health, academics, social life, and other responsibilities suffer from lack of sleep. When I observe such behavior, it is not surprising when these students are absent from class due to illness after physically wearing out their bodies. Given that they are not able to represent the best version of themselves in such a dazed state, students become emotional and depressed. Therefore, it is important to understand the physiological needs of our bodies and to protect adequate sleep time.

Rest and Solitude

Finding quiet moments of solitude to rest or sleep is difficult in a residential student learning community. Our bodies need time to rejuvenate, and this is where rest and sleep are vital. For introverts especially, this time away from people or distractions is necessary to thrive. Some students understand that getting to bed by a certain time is essential for them to function the next day, so they discipline themselves not to compromise their bed times. Other students schedule solitary moments of rest throughout the day by going back to their dorm rooms during a time when they know that their roommates have class, in order to enjoy a quiet space. *Our bodies need sleep and rest to function properly.* It is important to identify methods to manage our time carefully in order for these basic human needs to be met.

Guard and Maximize Study Time

Another challenge when managing time effectively in the new, socially rich college environment is guarding time to study and prepare sufficiently for classes. *Time is a rare commodity,* especially in college. Although students have elected to attend institutions of higher education to study, numerous temptations can quickly and easily overshadow academic life. Undergraduates must learn how to successfully balance their schoolwork with the countless social activities offered on campus, the ubiquitous presence of people, and mobile technologies that incessantly distract their attention.

Use the syllabi as a guide for key dates and time commitments

To begin establishing effective study habits, it is essential for students to read the syllabi carefully, while noting key due dates and estimating the time needed to properly complete specific assignments. Students will constantly be looking at the calendars of their respective courses to view schedules for the readings, papers, and projects so that they can schedule their time accordingly. *Maintaining a master calendar of all academic and social events will help students see a general overview of their time commitments.* Guarding time that is set aside to study is critical, and compromising study time will inevitably lead to late nights and substandard academic work.

Break down large, overwhelming tasks into smaller, manageable ones

It is daunting for college students to imagine completing a significant project such as a research paper, or studying for a lengthy period of time for a specific exam without interruption. In this case, it is recommended that students *transform larger blocks of study time into several shorter focused periods that are filled with small, manageable tasks to help increase productivity.* In the field of educational psychology, this strategy is referred to as chunking or scaffolding (Woolfolk, 2016). For example, in teaching, instructors scaffold students' work by dividing the elements of a research paper into several components, and then, providing support or tools to complete each section of the overall paper. In this way, students are able to reimagine one large, overwhelming task as a few, feasible fragments of activity.

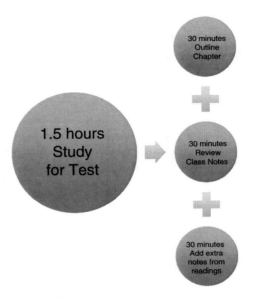

This is especially helpful in an age when mobile devices constantly detract from our ability to focus on one task for a long period of time. For example, if students are preparing for an exam, then they could begin with creating an outline, reviewing class notes, and following up with notes from the readings. Dividing study time into smaller components is an effective method to being more productive.

Attend classes

Students should attend classes regularly so that they can benefit from the knowledge gained from social learning. Given that attendance is not mandatory in many university courses, some students may choose not to attend class. But students should consider the consequences of this decision because *a great deal can be implicitly learned and retained through social learning activities employed in class*. Such methods include storytelling, pairing up with partners and sharing perspectives, collaborating in small groups, and seeing visual aids that are supported by insightful explanations. A social interaction in class may help students reinforce or clarify a key concept. Thus, protecting study time includes exercising the discipline to attend class regularly.

University students commonly assume that they will demonstrate the same outstanding cognitive abilities that they used to gain acceptance into the institution. Yet, if they are easily tempted by the myriad of social distractions in college, and do not establish effective study habits, then students' academic achievements will be negatively impacted. This remains one of the most profound perspectives of the college experience. The goal is not simply to succeed in classes and acquire outstanding grades. ***The valuable life lesson that college students learn is how to balance various key components of independent adult living, while simultaneously carrying out the academic responsibilities of a student successfully.***

Establish Social Life Boundaries

The social aspects of college life offer the greatest temptations to distract students from their academic commitments and deter them from getting adequate sleep. Formal functions may include university-sponsored activities such as athletic events, whereas informal activities might involve impromptu outings or casual conversations with roommates. The college environment is inundated with people and social activities. Although it is exciting and enticing to meet new people and participate in the social life of college, it is also important that students keep their eyes on the ultimate goal—which is to graduate from college. ***Participating in the social community in college is encouraged; however, it should not distract students so much that their academic standing is compromised.*** For instance, if a student has an exam at 8 a.m. on a Thursday, then socializing with roommates after dinner until midnight the evening before the exam is not ideal. As a result, preparing for the exam may not occur until after midnight, if at all, and one's sleep pattern and academic performance may also suffer from this poor choice of time management. In the end, if such patterns persist, and grades are consistently low, then students could conceivably be placed on academic probation, which would consequentially result in dismissal from the institution. College life is full of these types of scenarios where students must decide how to use their time wisely so that their academic and social lives will flourish simultaneously.

Putting it all Together: Sleep, Studies, Social Life + "Adulting"

Aside from the three main components of sleep, studies, and social life, college students will also need to carry out all the responsibilities of living on one's own. This is commonly referred to as "adulting," which involves the mundane chores affiliated with functioning daily as an independent adult. These duties include, but are not limited to, acquiring an income, managing finances, cleaning one's room, doing laundry, servicing a car, maintaining wellness (e.g., exercise, medical appointments, etc.), and shopping for essentials such as food or clothing. These simple, but necessary, tasks generally tend to take up more time than one realizes. In my personal experiences, I have found that one full day of the weekend can be dedicated to chores, such as house cleaning, laundry, grocery shopping, managing finances, and/or home maintenance. These responsibilities of living as an independent adult require time.

After combining a part-time job to the hours of studying and social activities, the formerly open and sparse schedule of an average college student is easily filled. Time has quickly become a rare commodity. The following table serves as a tangible representation of the valuable lesson that students will learn in college: ***Time is scarce; use it wisely***.

College Schedule with 15 Semester Units + Part-time Job + Social Activities

	Monday	Tuesday	Wednesday	Thursday	Friday
8–9 a.m.			Breakfast		
9–10 a.m.	Breakfast	SPAN 101	SPAN 101	SPAN 101	SPAN 101
10–11 a.m.	ENG 101 (10–11:30)	Work	Work	ENG 101 (10–11:30)	Work
11 a.m.–12 p.m.					
12–1 p.m.			Lunch		
1–2 p.m.	MATH 102	MATH 102	MATH 102	MATH 102	Work
2–3 p.m.	HUM 111 (2–3:30)	Work	Work	HUM 111 (2–3:30)	
3–4 p.m.					
4–5 p.m.	extras	ART 101		extras	
5–6 p.m.					
6–7 p.m.			Dinner		
7–8 p.m.		Study			extras
8–9 p.m.					
9–10 p.m.					
10 p.m. +			extras		

Methods to use time intentionally

College life marks a season of planning. Students will design a long-term plan to obtain their undergraduate degrees, and they will also create short-term goals to complete academic requirements during each semester or quarter. Undergraduates will be expected to have a clear grasp of their weekly time commitments, as well as their

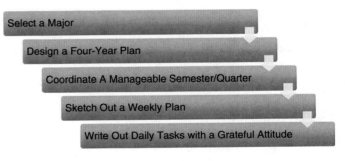

daily responsibilities. Each day, students are individually accountable for how they will use their time academically and socially, and these choices will directly impact both their long-term and short-term goals. So, how can college students begin to practice effective time management? The following section offers strategies that students can adopt to use time intentionally.

Big Picture Plans: Selecting a Major

One of the critical steps that students will make when managing time in college is committing to a major. Selecting a pathway to study will give students a general outline to follow during their typical four years in college. After researching various majors, students will be able to: (1) gauge their interests, (2) see if certain majors will take more or less than four years to complete, and (3) estimate the projected course load each semester or quarter to finish the degree requirements. For example, undergraduates pursuing a teaching credential will need to account for student teaching in their academic schedules, while those interested in the sciences may need to factor in extra lab times. Athletes, especially, will need to carefully consider which majors will most feasibly work with their tight practice and travel schedules. In these ways, *selecting a major prompts students to consider how time will be intentionally spent each semester.*

It is also highly recommended that students meet with academic advisors to uncover substitutions for particular requirements, or suggestions for summer options and study abroad programs, which may increase or decrease the length of a student's collegiate career. In my own experience, the small number of students who seek academic advice from faculty or staff have surprised me. Given the high cost of college tuition, *it would be in the students' best interest to consult an academic advisor to insure that the student optimizes the time spent in college.* Some institutions even place a hold on students' accounts, which requires students to meet with an advisor before registering for classes. It is important that students are aware of this requirement, and plan accordingly to release the hold before course registration opens. If students decide not to take advantage of academic advisors, then I suggest that they minimally discuss four-year plans with their peers and carefully read the academic catalog to gain insider knowledge on the college curriculum and major programs of study.

Designing a Four-Year Plan

After choosing a major, it is very helpful to make a list of the course requirements and design a four-year undergraduate plan. [*Table provided at the end of the chapter in "Applications."] This tangible schedule helps students to see how each semester or quarter will be intentionally spent. In college, students are required to complete a pre-determined set of General Education (G.E.) requirements, as well as courses outlined for the elected major. Students must consult both lists of courses when designing a four-year plan. By completing this exercise, students will also evaluate if all the necessary courses will fit into four years, or if extra time will need to be considered. On certain occasions, pre-collegiate credits gained from Advanced Placement (AP) testing or online courses may allow students to graduate earlier. Another reason to meet with academic advisors is because they will be more familiar with the rotation of course offerings in the curriculum, which will help with overall planning. Some college courses are only offered in either the fall or the spring. If a prerequisite is not met, then a student's schedule could be set off an entire year. In the end, *the four-year plan will determine the structure for each semester of their undergraduate career.*

Coordinate a Manageable Semester/Quarter

When designing the course load for each semester or quarter, there are a number of factors that students should consider. For example, freshmen will be the last group scheduled for course registration at most universities. As a result, many courses may be closed by the time that freshmen get online to select their courses. Several of my alumni have returned to my first-year seminar in the past to urge my students not to oversleep on the day that they register for classes and to be intentional about planning their course options ahead of time. *It is important that first-year students have backup options lined up in case their first choices when registering for classes are unavailable.* Lower level (100–200) G.E. courses are typically available for freshmen, whereas upper division courses are usually taken by upper classmen. *Doing the research before your course registration time is key to having a successful experience registering for classes.*

Next, it is important for students to *be mindful of the quality and quantity of courses that they will be taking each semester or quarter.* In college, four to five courses, or 12–16 units, comprise a typical load, but students should be careful to consider the rigor of the combination of courses if five classes are elected. Given that the difficulty of the course will vary, depending on factors such as the curriculum and the quality of the instructor, herein lies another reason for students to do research and gain insider knowledge from peers or professionals before selecting their courses. The following table represents a manageable five-course load, as well as a challenging five-course load:

Example of Manageable and Challenging Schedule

Manageable Schedule = 16 units • Eclectic mix of classes • Nice balance of reading assignments and content • Music course is light and only 2 units	1. Spanish 151 (4) 2. Math 102 (3) 3. Psychology 200 (3) 4. English 101 (4) 5. Piano 101 (2)
Challenging Schedule = 18 units • All solid courses • Heavy reading and writing in all courses • Overall, 2 more units than option above	1. Spanish 151 (4) 2. Humanities 101 (3) 3. Psychology 200 (3) 4. English 101 (4) 5. Biology (4)

Sketch Out a Weekly Plan

Once the semester starts and students begin attending classes, they will receive syllabi from all of their instructors, which will note significant dates for exams, quizzes, essays, assignments, and special projects. Undergraduates should write these noteworthy dates in a weekly or monthly planner right away. As the school year goes on, other important dates will also arise for extracurricular events, such as Greek formals, student club initiations, and athletic games. *Writing these special dates in a planner gives students an overview of their week, month, and semester/quarter.* Although it is also helpful and common to insert significant dates into mobile devices, it is more difficult to see a general summary on smaller devices such as Smartphones. Students can pilot a digital or handwritten approach, or do both, as they take this first step in planning for the short-term. *The key is to be aware of when milestones, or special events, occur within the calendar year, and then, to prioritize time accordingly.*

Students can develop a weekly schedule by creating a spreadsheet, or a simple table using any word processing software, and outlining the hours of each day. [A sample table has been provided at the end of this chapter.] Using colors to fill the cells will help symbolize the different elements represented on the table. This method is key in highlighting the various components of the week. Students should include the following items in their weekly schedules:

a. Class times and practice times (for athletes or performing arts)
b. Meals
c. Work hours
d. Exercise
e. Nonnegotiable study times
f. Social events, chores, personal appointments, and so on
g. Religious practices

It may seem astonishing to insert ordinary activities such as meal times in the weekly schedule; however, if students do not intentionally make time to eat, then they either: (1) do not eat, or (2) eat in class. *When time is not purposefully allotted in a schedule for a particular task, then the time to carry out the duty must be found somewhere else.* In this case, eating simultaneously during a class, when it is permissible, might have to be an option. Otherwise, students will remain hungry until a suitable time to eat is available. This is not an ideal solution, because the student's attention will be compromised.

It is important for students to understand that time is a finite resource; therefore, it should be used intentionally. Sketching out a weekly schedule is extremely helpful. This allows them to estimate their time commitments and visualize how they will purposefully utilize blocks of time in and out of the classroom. *Students should also post the schedule in their rooms, share it with roommates, and take a picture of it and add the weekly plan to a mobile device.* Having the schedule posted reminds students of their daily time commitments, and likewise, allows their peers to locate them, if needed. Having the weekly schedule readily available for reference is handy so that one can refer to their daily plan and utilize their time accordingly.

Write Out Daily Tasks with a Grateful Attitude

Undergraduates' daily responsibilities will vary, based upon their class schedules and extracurricular activities. There are numerous due dates and meetings to remember as well as multiple tasks to complete. It will be helpful to adopt a systematic method to be purposeful each day. *Writing down a to-do list in the morning helps people to use their time intentionally throughout the day* and is a strategy that business people strongly promote to increase productivity (Chowdhry, 2013; Mayberry, 2015). The checklist serves as a tangible representation of how time will be spent purposefully.

In my own routine, I have found that my workflow and productivity are greater when I write out a to-do list at the beginning of the day. I have combined this task list with the act of noting a few items for which I am thankful. Exercising a grateful attitude by writing down what we are thankful for is a practice that TED Talk speaker and CEO of Good Think, Inc., Shawn Achor, has implemented with businesses to help increase the work productivity and success of people. *In order to rewire our minds to focus on the positive, Achor (2011) recommended that we engage in exercises such as writing down what we are thankful for consecutively for at least 21 days.* By doing so, we can increase our happiness as well as our productivity.

Plan Ahead to Maximize Time

Given that time is finite and that the numerous tasks set before students might exceed the number of hours in a day, it is necessary to creatively and constructively plan ahead in order to maximize time. Knowing how to optimize time—and to be prepared to soak up time usefully—are critical skills. Although we all are granted the same amount of time daily, I have found that *individuals who are careful to use every minute of their time purposefully excel in and out of the classroom*. For example, if students are given time during class to work on a group project, then those who come prepared with the materials necessary to create the project in class will maximize their time together. They are the ones who leave with a completed project, rather than sitting idle and simply discussing what to do. They have thoughtfully carried out these discussions online beforehand and were productive in class. This critical element of planning allows the students to begin promptly working on their project while they are together. This is an example of optimizing class time.

Protect workflow

Scheduling events carefully in order to protect workflow is also a key to maximizing time. In my own experience while writing this book, I found that I needed full days to dedicate to my writing. Writing for only a few hours, and then, breaking to socialize or attend an appointment, would destroy my concentration and workflow. Even though it might initially appear that an appointment was only one hour, a substantial amount of time was spent traveling and refocusing. Therefore, Mondays and Tuesdays were generally committed to lengthy days of only writing. By scheduling meetings or appointments on Wednesdays, I protected my workflow and was able to be more productive. Similarly, students should be mindful of how they schedule their appointments or how often they check their mobile devices to optimize their productivity. If a student has a three-hour block of time on a Sunday afternoon without any school responsibilities or other commitments, then it would be best to guard that time for studying and preparing for the school week. *Thinking carefully about when appointments are scheduled, and preserving blocks of time without interruptions, will optimize your time.* Knowing how to schedule appointments within a day is key to workflow and higher productivity.

Multitask when appropriate

A clever strategy to optimize time is to kill two birds with one stone. Students can maximize their time by carefully scheduling and carrying out two activities at the same time *when appropriate*. The brain's ability to multitask is limited (as explained in chapter 7, technology), so undergraduates should be careful when giving their attention to two or more functions. One acceptable scenario depicts a student eating with a friend who has requested spending time together. Since the student already set aside an hour for breakfast or lunch in the daily plan, the mealtime is an ideal period to catch up with the friend. Exercising together could also be an option, if a work out time was established in the student's schedule. *The lesson here is to assess how time is spent throughout the day so that new appointments can be scheduled efficiently.*

I have personally encountered great success in this multitasking method and have seen how it has maximized my time. One year, I wanted to read several new books, but I did not see how I could fit in all the reading, given my impacted schedule. After evaluating my daily schedule, I realized that I could listen to audio books for free using the Overdrive app during my 40-minute one-way commute to work. I was able to transform some dead, aimless time in the car into a useful, productive commute. By simply supplementing my drive to work with an audiobook, I completed reading ten books in one year. This was a creative way to optimize my time, and I encourage students to think imaginatively in this same way.

Be prepared to soak up idle time

Throughout the day, there may be moments when students surprisingly and delightfully encounter unexpected downtime. These open times may consist of a few minutes or larger blocks. In any case, it is important to utilize this idle time mindfully. If your bodies need rest, then use these occasions as treasured moments of solitude. When students are prepared with the necessary materials, these instances can be transformed into constructive time. I recommend that students place a set of Thank You notes in their cars or in their backpacks. **Brief moments of time are perfect for writing out a quick and thoughtful Thank You note.** Carrying some form of reading in the car, a briefcase, or a purse is also very handy. With mobile technologies, reading emails or checking social media has evolved into a culturally accepted way to spend unscheduled downtime throughout the day. Although there are occasions when our mobile devices conveniently allow us to complete tasks, they can also lure us into mindless activities for too long. **People should be cautious and spend their time purposefully, rather than aimlessly when it unexpectedly appears.** By being prepared, and carefully thinking about how to use our energy, we all can soak up time throughout the day in a productive manner.

Conclusion

In truth, if someone asked me what the most important lesson is that one learns in college, I would unhesitatingly respond that it is how to manage time effectively. Time is the resource that all college students are given, but how each person utilizes it underpins how the varying levels of achievement, effort, performance, relationships, and confidence are determined. The critical life lessons that underlie the skill of managing time effectively are: (1) acknowledging priorities, (2) understanding boundaries, (3) managing self-discipline, and (4) following through on commitments. Living independently is one step in your adult life, and learning how to thrive independently rests on your ability to make decisions that will reflect your goals, effort, and standards. Managing your time efficiently will set a solid foundation for your success in college and beyond.

Reflective Summary

Discussions

1. Describe your schedule in high school and in college. Share some similarities and differences. What has been the most surprising aspect of your college schedule?

2. What time do you need to get to bed by to function at an optimum level the next day? What is your ideal time to wake up in the morning?

3. Study time, social life, and sleep. Which of these three elements do you think you would most likely compromise first? Why?

4. What type of chores have you assumed in college that you did not do before? (e.g., doing laundry, cooking, maintaining car, etc.)

5. An appointment that you have is running late, so you have 20 minutes of unexpected time. What are some ways that you could use this time productively?

Applications

1. Write a list of items for which you are grateful. Do this each day before our class meets again. Describe how this practice affected your attitude or work productivity during the week.

2. Create a weekly schedule, inserting your classes, work, practice times for athletics, meals, nonnegotiable study times, and social hours. Be sure to use colors to represent the different elements of your schedule.

	Monday	Tuesday	Wednesday	Thursday	Friday
8–9 a.m.					
9–10 a.m.					
10–11 a.m.					
11 a.m.–12 p.m.					
12–1 p.m.					
1–2 p.m.					
2–3 p.m.					
3–4 p.m.					
4–5 p.m.					
5–6 p.m.					
6–7 p.m.					
7–8 p.m.					
8–9 p.m.					
9–10 p.m.					
10 p.m. +					

3. Make a list of the general education requirements you must still complete. Then, make a list of courses from a particular major that you are interested in pursuing or have already declared.

4. Fill out the four-year plan using the given template.

Four-Year Plan

Student Name: Concentration/Minor:
Major:

Freshman Fall _____	Spring _____	Summer _____

Sophomore Fall _____	Spring _____	Summer _____

Junior Fall _____	Spring _____	Summer _____

Senior Fall _____	Spring _____	Summer _____

Fifth Year (if necessary) Fall	Spring	Summer _____

CHAPTER 5

Wellness

Practicing Healthy Habits to Preserve Mental Health

"Health is a state of complete physical, mental and social
well-being and not merely the absence of disease or infirmity."

— *World Health Organization*

According to the executive summary of the 2016 survey completed by 80,139 undergraduates for the American College Health Association, feelings of sadness, loneliness, depression, and anxiety prevail among college students. When asked to describe their mental health within the last 12 months of the survey, students reported the following:

- ***86 percent felt overwhelmed by all they had to do***
- 66 percent felt very sad
- 60.8 percent felt very lonely
- 59 percent felt overwhelming anxiety
- 37.5 percent felt so depressed that it was difficult to function.

After comparing the data from the spring 2011 survey with the spring 2016 survey, Petersen (2016) also revealed that anxiety among undergraduates is up by 11.6 percent and depression is up 10.7 percent nationwide.

It is alarming and concerning that the mental health of young people is suffering; however, this is not surprising, given the steep learning curve that students experience when transitioning from adolescence to adulthood while in college. Although students enroll in universities to pursue academic degrees, the college experience offers much more than simply growing the intellectual mind. College opens the door to a world of newness—international students have been transported to a *new* country, domestic students may have moved to a *new* state, first-year and transfer students have enrolled in a *new* school filled with *new* people, residential students will live in a *new* dormitory with *new* roommates, and the list of *new* factors goes on and on. All of these novel elements can be exciting, but they can also contribute to anxiety, stress, and sadness. Forming habits to maintain a healthy mental state so that students can make good choices and thrive during this life-changing transition is critical.

Preserving wellness through meeting needs of college students

Results from the 2012 survey of the Association for University and College Center Directors confirmed that the mental health of college students is a growing concern. "***Anxiety continues to be the most predominant presenting concern among college students (41.6%), followed by depression (36.4%), and relationship problems (35.8%)***" (Mistler, Reetz, Krylowicz, & Barr, 2012, p. 5). The research literature also revealed that symptoms of these illnesses relate to the basic physical levels of an individual's needs being compromised in some way. For instance, students who suffer from depression frequently exhibit irregular sleep patterns or unhealthy diets. Missing home and feeling lonely in the new college environment are also likely emotions that undergraduates will experience. In this case, the basic emotional need of belonging is not satisfied, so the student is left feeling sad and isolated. The transition to college is a challenging time, and ***the university setting is an ideal breeding ground for feelings of inadequacy or isolation*** that can negatively impact students' mental wellness.

Maslow's Hierarchy: Understanding the Basic Needs of Human Beings

In the world of psychology, Maslow's hierarchy is a framework used to explain the motivational needs of human beings (Woolfolk, 2016). People are motivated to fulfill their basic physiological needs before advancing to satisfy higher-level needs such as safety, love/belonging, self-esteem, and self-actualization. The structure of the pyramid helps learners to remember the hierarchical format. Similarly, the transformational journey of a college student follows the premise of Maslow's hierarchy. It is unlikely that the fulfillment of needs follows such a clear,

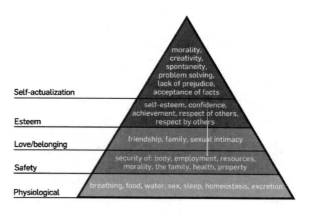

linear progression as Maslow implies. Still, the idea that greater success or healthier states of being are achieved when the basic levels are met first is sensible.

Understanding the Needs of College Students

The modified hierarchy presented here outlines the needs of college students. It incorporates the theme of life lessons that students will face as they navigate their college years. The labels for each level similarly correspond to the ideas presented in Maslow's hierarchy. Undergraduates will learn to independently care for their basic *physical* necessities: sleep, food, exercise, laundry, personal hygiene. Then, they will assess and address their *emotional* needs; having friends, belonging to a community, feeling loved, valued, and appreciated. Next, they will fulfill

Identifying purpose; Understanding vocation — **spiritual**

Academic knowledge; forming a worldview; shaping beliefs, morals, ethics — **intellectual**

Friends, relationships, belonging, feeling loved, valued, & appreciated — **emotional**

Food, sleep, exercise, clothing, personal hygiene — **physical**

their *intellectual* purposes: learning academic knowledge, informing their worldview, shaping their beliefs, morals, and ethics. Finally, students may actualize their *spiritual* commitments: identifying their greater purpose or understanding their vocation.

The following list offers a sample set of questions that students commonly ask when contemplating their various needs and preserving their wellness in a new college community.

Physical: How will I sleep if my new roommate stays up late at night?
Physical: What will I eat if I do not like what is served in the cafeteria or if my classes run consecutively for 6 hours during the day?
Emotional: How will I decompress as an introvert if there are people everywhere all the time?
Emotional: How will I make new friends? What if I do not fit into the community?
Intellectual: How will I decide upon a major if I do not know what I want to study?
Intellectual: What are my own political, moral, and ethical beliefs?
Spiritual: What faith tradition am I committed to and why?
Spiritual: How will I fulfill my life's purpose?

The theory suggests that students will progress through a series of stages before attaining a level of self-fulfillment. However, the reality is that there are occasions when optimal conditions are not in place, and students still experience some form of success. For example, after skipping a meal and disregarding the body's physical need for nourishment, as well as pulling an all-nighter and ignoring the body's need for sufficient sleep, it is still possible for a student to earn a high grade on an exam. But, this comes at a cost. The student's wellness has been compromised in the process, and over time, these practices will lead to burnout and an unhealthy mental state.

Methods to maintain wellness

The introduction to college life and independent living can be jarring if undergraduates do not cultivate healthy habits. In addition to caring for their physical bodies so that they can minimize illness, students should also consider how they will protect their mental health. This is especially necessary given the highly intense, emotionally charged climate of college. ***Without protecting*** *the basic physical needs of safety, sleep, diet, and exercise, students will run down physically and burn out emotionally in college.* I have found that whenever people begin a new chapter in life, such as getting married, having a baby, or going to college, they are inundated with bits of advice. It is often difficult to recall the most valuable wisdom that was shared. In the following section, I have curated the most valuable tips that will benefit students as they navigate the challenges of maintaining their mental wellness during their college years.

Caring for Your Basic Physical Needs: Safety, Sleep, Diet, and Exercise

Living in a new community requires a great deal of adjustment. One of the first shocking revelations that college students will experience is the unique dynamics of living away from home in a small space with strangers. Beginning college is a formative experience that spawns a sense of responsibility and self-sufficiency that traditional students typically do not encounter while residing at home. This introduction to independent living also opens the door to numerous life lessons that will lay a foundation for maintaining physical wellness.

Address roommate problems immediately

It is essential for students to feel safe and to have a calm place to sleep and rest. If there is stress and strife in one's living conditions, then there is no safe place to relax and rejuvenate. Therefore, it is important to address any roommate conflicts immediately. Practicing the communication skills that are offered in chapter 3 of this text might be a logical first step in bringing up an issue. However, *if the situation calls for university personnel to be consulted, then students should take advantage of this support system*.

Sleep

Acquiring adequate sleep is vital to optimal academic performance and a healthy emotional state. *30.9 percent of the undergraduates who completed the spring 2016 National College Health Assessment reported that their sleep difficulties were "traumatic or difficult to handle"* (American College Health Association, 2016, p. 15). When I speak at freshman orientations, this is one of the main pieces of advice that I always share with incoming students: **Sleep. It's that simple.**

As a new parent, many veteran mothers advised me to sleep when my baby slept so that I could rejuvenate my body to keep up with the demands of motherhood. Although it was difficult to heed this advice daily, I did pause to nap when I felt like I was reaching burnout. I felt comforted knowing that someone had encouraged me to sleep while my baby rested, and this somehow alleviated any guilt that I unnecessarily put on myself for resting. In this same way, I encourage college students to evaluate when they have reached their limits and to give their bodies a break when needed. Do not give in to constant all-nighters and late nights! *Be the rebel in your dormitory or apartment—Sleep!*

As students settle into a routine, they will assess and identify how much sleep they will need to be alert and thrive. Clinicians state that it is ideal to get eight hours of sleep, but this may be unrealistic for college students, especially if they are not disciplined. Managing one's time carefully is key to guarding sufficient sleep time. If time is not used properly throughout the day, then sleep is a basic physical need that is typically compromised first. Inadequate sleep will lead to physical illness, poor academic performance, or depression, so it is vital to guard sleep time.

Establish a healthy diet

Navigating meal times successfully and selecting nutritional options and appropriate portions when living independently are essential in maintaining a healthy diet. Although it is typical for college students to skip meals or to sustain their bodies regularly with unhealthy and quick options such as pizza and soda, these decisions do not provide students with the essential nutrients needed to thrive. ***Making a habit of walking to the most convenient stations in the cafeteria, such as the pizza counter or the soda fountain, is not wise***. Students should be mindful of their daily intake of fruits and vegetables and be intentional about choosing healthy options regularly. One strategy is to set goals to consume a fruit or vegetable at particular meals. Another practical method is to substitute water for soda to keep the body well hydrated. ***Carrying a refillable water bottle reminds students to drink water continuously throughout the day and supports the increase of fluid intake.*** Filling our bodies with healthy food and staying hydrated optimizes the brain's functionality.

Avoid drugs and drink responsibly

College students should be aware of the negative impact of drugs and alcohol upon their cognitive abilities. The undergraduate years represent a season when students will be tempted by these elements, especially given that young adults will reach the legal drinking age during this period. The ease of accessibility and ubiquitous presence of drugs and alcohol on college campuses cannot be denied. However, avoiding drugs and learning how to drink responsibly will positively impact the mind, body, and spirit of students. As a faculty member, I have served on disciplinary committees where illegal drugs or irresponsible alcohol usage led to severe sanctions that changed the trajectory of students' undergraduate careers. It is important that young people make smart choices in these regards so that they do not compromise their lives, others' lives, or their academic standing with the institution.

Exercise regularly

If exercise is not built into students' schedules, then it is easy to ignore. Many students may have played sports regularly and had a consistent training schedule in high school, but chose not to continue playing sports at the collegiate level. Given that the formerly embedded system of exercise has vanished, students must consider how they will engage in exercise while in college. Intramural sports are a popular option among students. Inserting a regular walk during the day, a hike on the weekends, or a workout in one's daily plan is necessary to keep the brain alert and to exercise the heart muscle. Only 20.5 percent of undergraduates in the spring 2016 health assessment reported engaging in moderate-to-intense cardio or aerobic exercise for at least 30 minutes in a one-week time span (American College Health Association, 2016). Exercise is a key element that will enhance the body's ability to be alert, awake, and healthy.

Fill Your Emotional Tank

The college years are a very emotionally charged time in young people's lives. Leaving what is familiar, being separated from family and friends, developing authentic, life-giving relationships, and finding your niche in a new community are all processes that require a lot of energy. Being a university student also marks a formational period when young adults are confronted with real-life issues such as their sexuality, drug and alcohol usage, living with roommates, and dating—all which impact people's mental health. It is easy for students to feel emotionally depleted from being constantly surrounded by people and persistently making efforts to leave positive impressions upon others. The fast-paced, intense climate of college can be exhausting and students' emotional tanks need to somehow be filled regularly.

Identify methods to regain energy

Undergraduates should identify how they will rest and recharge in an environment that breeds overcommitted, active people. Before entering college, students may have never contemplated if they are an introvert or an extrovert. Assessing if you gain energy from being alone (like most introverts) or by interacting with people (like most extroverts) is a helpful step in understanding how you find peace or joy and feel relaxed or energized. It is important to schedule these strategies into your planner regularly. Filling a schedule with constant activity can be easily done in college because of the myriad of activities available everywhere; however, our human bodies need rest and the opportunity to recharge, especially while navigating an environment that is filled with students with heightened emotions and overcommitted schedules.

I once bumped into a former student in the halls of our university and noticed that she had a terrible cold. Her sinuses were congested, and she appeared very fatigued. She shared that she had been ill for a long time and could not seem to get better. I recognized that the student was very active in the college community and was an exceptional student; therefore, she had very little time to rest or slow down. Given that the student's family lived in another state, I knew that she had not enjoyed a home-cooked meal or been in a home for quite some time. I genuinely believed that this young lady just needed some downtime to restore her body. So, I invited her and a friend to our home, prepared them a meal, gave them a space to do their homework, and allowed them to sit comfortably on the couch with blankets while watching television. My student was able to rest that evening, and soon, her body began to restore itself. Later, I ran into her at the university again, and she shared that she felt much better after experiencing some downtime that night off-campus. There are limits to the human body's capabilities. If we are not mindful of preserving our wellness, then our bodies will become sick and shut down. It is important to identify ways to take care of ourselves purposefully.

Consult professionals if needed

Universities recognize the stress and emotional burdens that students carry and provide free counseling center services and programs for young people. Petersen (2016) confirmed that there is a surge in counseling centers treating college students, with reports noting an increase as high as 43 percent in the number of college students treated in the last 5 years. The transition from adolescence to adulthood is challenging, and sometimes, it is helpful to receive advice from a professional. Family troubles, personal trauma, death of a family member or friend, relationship difficulties—these issues may all surface during college. Students are encouraged to take advantage of counseling center services to help navigate these problems, and their anonymity is ensured in the process. Having a counselor visit my first-year seminar class each semester to outline the services that the center offers has been greatly beneficial. Each time afterwards, at least one of my students has written me a personal note to affirm that he or she appreciated the reminder of the counseling center services and was encouraged to reach out for professional help.

Wellness Affects Academic Performance

College studies are rigorous. Preparing projects, speeches, presentations, keeping up with readings, writing essays, completing homework assignments, and exams or quizzes can induce anxiety and overcome students with stress. In addition to all of this, students must also learn to balance sports practices, athletic games, travel time, work, and extracurricular activities with their academic life. Given these numerous commitments, it is not surprising that 86 percent of undergraduates felt overwhelmed with all that they had to do (American College Health Association, 2016). Additionally, college students reported that *anxiety (24.4%), depression (16.2%), sleep (22.2%), and stress (33.8%) all negatively impacted their academic performance* (American College Health Association, 2016). In my work with university students, the most common breakdown that I see among first-year college students stems from their inability to achieve their true level of academic abilities because of poor choices in time management. As a result, they are disappointed in themselves because they have not completed an assignment or done as well on an exam to represent their true potential. This cyclical behavior leads to stress, sadness, and great anxiety. Therefore, students should adopt the following strategies to increase greater academic success while simultaneously preserving their mental wellness.

Manage time wisely

When students pause to consider why they did not perform successfully in a particular class, more often than not, the reason can be attributed to poor time management. Typically, students who have not completed my class assignments or have turned in poor quality work simply did not manage their schedules wisely to devote adequate time to their studies. They could be working too much, not getting sufficient sleep, socially overcommitted, or a combination of these factors. After students receive their first grades, they will either accept their level of academic achievement, or they will make changes to improve it. In most cases, low grades prompt students to carefully analyze how their time management has impacted their academic performance.

Forgive yourself

As students learn to navigate the intense schedule of college life, mistakes will be made. Students will oversleep, miss appointments, forget assignments, or inadequately prepare for an exam. There is a steep learning curve in managing all of the responsibilities of college life, and making a mistake is inevitable. ***Forgive yourself.*** As a first-year seminar professor for the past six years, I have visions of students from each year who have come to me in tears while expressing their disappointment after receiving their first poor grade. This moment typically coincides with a student's emotional meltdown due to their overcommitted schedules and lack of sleep. After experiencing this moment, I encourage the students to learn from the incident, make adjustments, and move forward. A mistake will not define you unless you allow it to do so. ***Growth comes from learning from the error and correcting it.*** But, sometimes students are so disappointed in their poor behavior and performance that it is difficult for them to be lifted out of their depressed mental states to continue. It is helpful to talk to someone for extra support. Then forgive yourself, make changes, and press on.

Bounce back with great intention

If students seek to improve their standing in a class after making some mistakes, it is important for them to show the professor that they intend to bounce back with great intention. ***Professors appreciate resilient students***. Make class a priority. Go to office hours. Meet with the professor or teaching assistant. Go to a study session. Seek professional help if needed. Turn things around. Feeling overwhelmed, stressed, and sad will persist if changes are not purposefully made after a concern has been identified. In other words, ***actions speak louder than words***.

Managing the Stress of Life's Larger Questions

As undergraduates determine their goals and begin to shape their personal belief systems, they will experience a wide range of emotions. The college years can be a stressful time for those who are uncertain about their futures. I have met with many students who feel overwhelmed and anxious because they do not know what to major in during their initial years in college. This is a critical decision that can impact the trajectory of their lives, and students may feel panicky if they have not committed to a major.

As students begin to grow and learn in college, I see them questioning their beliefs, their faith, their morals, and their ethics. This process can lead to feelings of disillusionment. For example, a college student who takes a religion class may be exposed to the details of a faith tradition, which he or she did not realize existed before. Such a revelation of knowledge is empowering, but the information may challenge the student's personal faith and cause the individual to question and defend the heritage of his or her own belief system. This experience can be emotionally taxing and often stressful, especially if it leads to students adopting beliefs that are different than their family or friends. Students will encounter moments like this in their undergraduate development when they may feel stressed or anxious trying to answer some serious life questions.

The following list offers a sample of life questions that college students grapple with during their college experience:

1. **Academics**: How will I choose my major? Why did I choose that major? Will my family approve that I picked that major? How will I use my academic knowledge in my future career?

2. **Faith**: Why am I committed to a particular faith tradition? Or, why do I not believe in a higher power? Do I believe what I believe because of my upbringing, or do I genuinely and personally believe it? How do I envision fulfilling my purpose in life?
3. **Politics**: What are my political beliefs? How has my family influenced my beliefs? What have I learned in college that has changed my worldview? How can I make a difference in the injustice that I see in the world today?
4. **Morals/Ethics**: How do I base my decisions for right or wrong? How has my upbringing affected my code of ethics?

These are rhetorical questions that require careful consideration and deep reflection, though they do not have any one possible solution. I included these questions in this text because students may not anticipate facing these life lessons initially during their college journey, and the list may give them an idea of what may lie ahead. The beginning of college is filled with the excitement of leaving home and addressing the lower levels of the needs hierarchy: getting along with a roommate, being comfortable in a new living space, sleeping, eating, and making friends. But in the course of learning and maturation, college students will advance to higher levels of the needs pyramid, which will call them to apply their intellectual knowledge for a higher purpose. Forming these advanced thoughts and beliefs requires a great deal of emotional and intellectual energy, so it is helpful to gain the support of a mentor during this process.

Find a mentor

One of the strongest predictors of academic and overall adjustment in college is a relationship with a mentor (Lenz, 2014). Studies show that the quality of the mentor relationship was more important than the identity of the mentor (Lenz, 2014; McGuire & Reger, 2003). Therefore, a family member, upperclassman, university representative, or other community members could fill the role of the mentor, which broadens the pool. Having an advisor who can support you throughout the academic and social challenges experienced in college is beneficial in numerous ways. Scheduling regular meetings with a mentor helps students share their anxiety, stress, questions, and experiences with someone who can affirm, guide, and suggest methods for coping and self-care. In my first-year seminars, my students see the great value of identifying a mentor early in their undergraduate careers. Adjusting to college can be particularly emotional and difficult in the first semester, and a mentor can be a support and guide through this challenging time. Identifying a mentor at the university also has the advantage of connecting undergraduates immediately to the college community. This will be extremely important when letters of recommendation and academic advising are needed in addition to emotional support. My college mentor continues to be a part of my life as a sage advisor and has been a constant resource of peace and calmness to help alleviate stress during difficult times throughout my life.

Conclusion

There is a great deal of pressure and intense emotion involved in pursuing a college degree. Stress and high levels of anxiety are a part of the process early in the admissions season, and depression can seep in during the adjustment phase. It is clear from the research and from students' anecdotal experiences that the intense college schedule can be overwhelming and that support mechanisms need to be in place to help students navigate this emotional time. In the end, the ultimate goal should not simply be that students graduate with a college degree; instead, it is vital for students to identify and practice effective strategies that will help them thrive physically, emotionally, intellectually, and spiritually in life. By doing so, they will, in turn, model healthy habits of living for other adults to emulate, so that the increasing numbers of people who suffer from mental illness will be reduced.

Reflective Summary

Discussions

1. Describe the last time when you participated in a new activity or visited a new place. How did you feel? What helped you to have an enjoyable experience? What do you think could have improved your experience?
2. What is something that you enjoy doing every day to prevent stress or make you happy?
3. What kind of advice have people given you to help you in your college journey?

Applications

1. Of the items listed below, rate how you believe it impacts your stress level on a 1–5 scale (5 being the highest).

   _____ Pulling an all-nighter   _____ Forgetting to do your homework
   _____ Failing a quiz   _____ Oversleeping
   _____ Leaving your phone at home   _____ Not getting along with your roommate
   _____ Relationship breakup   _____ Responding to emails and texts
   _____ Social media   _____ Missing class
   _____ Family problems at home   _____ Finances
2. List 5 things you enjoy doing to relax or regain energy.
3. Share 3 pictures that bring you joy. Explain why they make you happy.

CHAPTER 6

Public Speaking

#whatisthepoint: Designing Presentations with a Purpose

"A talk is a voyage with a purpose, and it must be charted. The man who starts out going nowhere, generally gets there."

— *Dale Carnegie*

Public speaking is an art. A blank canvas of time is given to a presenter, and how the individual utilizes it can leave the audience filled with either endless reflections from the message or completely unchanged by the experience. Colleges and universities acknowledge the useful skill of public speaking and often require a speech course as part of the general education requirements. It is also common for professors to assign presentations regularly in classes, so mastering the skill of giving presentations is valuable.

When developed and executed successfully, presentations can be inspiring and impactful, and when done poorly, they are pedantic and painful. If students enter college without ever having been taught how to give a presentation effectively, then they are left to navigate their way through these dark moments in a classroom without a light. With the few essential tips presented in this chapter, an ordinary presentation can be transformed into an extraordinary one. In college and beyond, several opportunities to make an oral presentation will arise, and being equipped with the fundamental skills necessary to deliver a memorable and polished presentation will set an individual apart in the classroom and in the workforce.

Presentations: The good, the bad, and the forgotten

During my 26 years in education and even beyond that, I have witnessed countless presentations and have been inspired by many superbly designed and well-executed speeches that have left me thinking about the experience long after the presentations have ended. Typically, these talented presenters are ones who have brilliantly combined their charisma, pedagogy, knowledge, and presentation design in a dynamic way. The skillful execution of their presentations has fueled my passion to learn more about how to deliver such an impactful message. Often, I have been compelled to open the notepad on my phone to jot down the appealing traits of their presentations during their speech, while on other occasions, I did not need to do this because the presentation was so outstanding that the speaker had already seared the information into my implicit memory. Such marvelously designed presentations not only delivered memorable and clear instruction, but also left me feeling inspired.

I have also been incredibly discouraged by poorly executed presentations, and am disappointed when students, faculty, or people in general, attend a lecture or event where someone has spoken for 10 minutes to 4 hours or more, and the audience cannot recall what the main point of the presentation was. It boggles my mind when a presentation lacks so many critical elements that it leaves the audience confused, disengaged, and unchanged from the experience. I feel equally, if not more frustrated, when I think of the numerous presentations I have attended over the years in various settings such as classrooms, faculty meetings, keynote addresses, graduation ceremonies, church sermons, and business meetings, where educated individuals have delivered presentations and I am left asking myself in the first few minutes, *"What is the point?"*

To my dismay, I have routinely exited the majority of these occasions with the lingering question of "What WAS the point?" and have felt frustrated when trying to summarize what the purpose of the speech was that I had witnessed. As a teacher, my frustration sparked a genuine desire to help my students, as well as my colleagues, to improve their presentation skills so that ineffective presentations could be minimized in the future. While observing various speeches, I routinely took notes to identify the elements in impressive presentations that contributed to their success and to highlight the errors found in unsuccessful presentations that could have been easily corrected. What I found most interesting was the fact that the common attributes of the well-designed presentations were fundamental, yet regularly omitted in a majority of the presentations that I witnessed. The audience and I appreciated when positive energy was established at the onset of a presentation, when a clear purpose statement was shared, and when the speaker did not simply read their slides. Similarly, the elements that I noted in the unsuccessful presentations were ordinary mistakes that could have been avoided. These characteristics include, but are not limited to, presentations packed with *too much content, slides filled with excessive text, poor timing, no closure, or a weak outline*. The point here is that *the art of delivering a clear and memorable presentation is teachable; it can be learned.*

Studying the design of a presentation has also become an automatic reflex for me as a maven, or a seeker of knowledge (Gladwell, 2002). I strive to know how to design presentations with a purpose, and how to teach others to do the same. Additionally, in my work with teachers and professionals of all levels, I see great value in this body of knowledge because it serves as a practical and useful resource for students, teachers, and other professionals who are required to design and execute presentations in their respective workplaces.

When creating and giving a presentation, the presenter essentially becomes a teacher. As a teacher educator, I see many clear commonalities shared between good teaching and effective presentations. One does not need to possess the title of "teacher" to be a teacher. Students take on the role of teacher when giving presentations in their classrooms, or even outside the classroom in their faith institutions or with their student-led organizations. Presentations are shared in tiny, intimate gatherings such as coffee houses, college dormitories, or seminar rooms where two or more people gather, formal business settings where small groups meet, and in large college lecture halls and professional conferences where thousands come together to learn from one another. In all of these occasions, individuals have been assigned or have volunteered to give a presentation to a specific group of people, or to teach them. Within the discipline of educational psychology stem the essential skills that presenters should always consider when delivering presentations with a purpose.

The audience: Optimizing the functionality of the human brain

My passion for education fuels my desire to better understand how to maximize the brain's full potential so that learning can be optimized in any setting. I strive to know how I can present information in a compelling way that leaves lasting impressions upon learners. I want the students in my classroom and the people in the audiences of schools and conferences where I present to leave the venue feeling challenged, changed, and different from my words. I constantly aim to present my material in a memorable way so that my audience does not have to struggle to recall the purpose in my presentation. What I have learned is that if I am asking the audience to engage their brains as they consume the knowledge or information that I am presenting, then I should look to the field of scientific research to see how the brain works and use this knowledge to my advantage when designing presentations. The essential tips shared in this chapter are based upon brain research and how its principles can be applied when creating and delivering impressive and memorable presentations. After sharing this lesson about how to deliver effective presentations with my first-year seminars over the past six years, I have consistently received positive comments about the great value that students have found in these helpful tips. Alumni have frequently returned to share that they have applied the principles learned from this lesson in their other courses. The art of giving a clear and engaging oral presentation is a skill that is relevant and valuable in numerous settings in your college experience and beyond.

Start with the basics: Introduction, content, conclusion

It has been said that people fear public speaking more than death, so the thought of composing an eloquent or memorable speech may be daunting for those who possess this anxiety when giving oral presentations. I recommend initiating the process by dividing the content into three basic stages: *(1) the introduction, (2) the content, and (3) the conclusion*. Within each of these stages, I suggest considering some fundamental tips when designing and delivering a compelling and clear presentation.

Introduction: How to Begin an Effective Presentation

Within the first 30 seconds of a presentation, the speaker must capture the audience's attention and set a positive tone and solid foundation for a speech, or the audience will be left disengaged, confused, and/or uninterested. First, the presenter must determine a clear purpose statement to share during the introduction. The human brain thrives when having purpose. Learners want to know what the point of a presentation is, and people are more invested when their brains are engaged with an intentional goal. Defining the purpose of the presentation will also help organize the content of the presentation. Additionally, our brains function optimally when we are in a positive mood. Therefore, integrating elements at the beginning of a speech that promote a happy learning environment is key to launching a successful presentation. The following section offers suggestions on how to address these two vital steps of the introduction: *(1) composing a clear purpose statement, and (2) creating a positive setting for learning.*

#Hashtags—Identifying and summarizing key points

In our millennial age, new technical acronyms and symbols have evolved as we adopt the latest tools and learn to navigate a digital world. Hashtags are used as: (1) labels for categorizing information, and as (2) summative, witty remarks. For instance, a hashtag could simply categorize all tweets or photos related to a particular event such as #Olympics2016, or a hashtag could accompany a tweet or photo to add an amusing comment. For example, when describing the overcrowded rooms at a conference with one band of text, one could add #deathbyclaustrophobia. I appreciate hashtags because they help organize information, and they encapsulate a main point that an author is trying to convey in a brief chain of text that is often accompanied by sarcasm or humor. Succinct. Clear. Purposeful. In this same way, I encourage presenters to think about what hashtags might be used to summarize the main points of their presentation. *If an audience member cannot create a few hashtags automatically from a presentation, then the purpose of the presentation was not clear*. I have intentionally included a hashtag in the title of this chapter and throughout its content to reinforce key points, to remind presenters to organize their material well, and to make their content direct, clear, and with a tinge of humor, which audiences always appreciate.

#Purpose—State and reinforce the main point

In teaching, I have witnessed countless times when students have entered the room asking, "What are we doing today?" Sometimes, there is one brilliant individual who also poses the question, "Are we doing anything important today?" That is always a favorite student inquiry among teachers. If we step back to consider what students are truly asking, we see that they want to uncover the purpose of the class time. This reinforces the fact that *our brains seek the meaning of the instruction.*

#Agenda—Include a visual aid of the purpose and agenda

As a teacher educator, it is a routine practice to instruct prospective teachers about how to develop an effective lesson plan. One of the most important steps in this exercise is to state clearly the objective of the lesson. This is similar to communicating the purpose of a presentation to an audience. It is important for teachers to be able to articulate the objective of their lessons. Now with the standardized education movement, teachers often feel compelled to write their objectives on the board for students to see. A common practice that I routinely enact when beginning a class is simply writing the agenda of topics that will be covered during that particular day on the board for all to see. A typical agenda looks like this:

1. Announcements and upcoming due dates
2. Quiz—Chapter 4
3. Brief review of last lesson—Cognitive Psychology (Piaget & Vygotsky)
4. New lesson—Moral Development (Erikson, Kohlberg, Gilligan)
5. Guest speaker—High school counselor

This may seem like a basic task, but its effects should not be underestimated. This answers the question for that student who walks in the room asking or thinking, "What are we going to do today?" Whether people are enrolled in an academic course or attending a professional meeting, sharing the outline for the time that will be spent together eases tension, focuses efforts, and communicates purpose.

For other occasions, such as a student presentation or a public speech, an ordinary way to share the agenda is to include a visual aid that shares what will be accomplished during the presentation. Using a simple method such as projecting a slide that states the agenda is useful and effective.

State the agenda

If a visual aid of the agenda is not included, then the presenter should minimally state the agenda in the first few minutes of the presentation. This strategy will still communicate the purpose of the presentation to the audience and accomplish this fundamentally important objective. For example, the speaker could communicate one of the following statements:

a. "Today, I will be sharing with you . . ."
b. "During our time together today, we will . . ."
c. "Before you leave today, you will be able to . . ."

Stating the purpose of a presentation is a simple, yet vital step that should be included in the introduction of any successful presentation.

#Positives—Create a positive learning environment

TED Talk Speaker and positive psychology advocate Shawn Achor (2011) confirmed that the brain's functional abilities are maximized when it is in a positive state, as opposed to feeling neutral or stressed. Neurologist and educator Judy Willis (2011) also validated this assertion after researching brain functionality as it relates particularly to the writing process. Willis found, "The brain scans of subjects learning in supportive and emotionally pleasurable situations show facilitated passage of information through the amygdala up to the higher cognitive brain, so learning associated with positive emotion is retained longer. Stress, however, determines if the intake is sent to that lower reactive brain." Knowing this information, presenters should consider how they can *infuse positive energy* in their presentations so that optimal learning conditions can be created. Below are suggestions for developing a positive setting for learning when designing and delivering memorable and effective presentations.

#PlayMusic—Use songs to manage the audience's energy

Music is one of the most underutilized tools when giving presentations. The tempo, rhythm, and beat of a song can help uplift a mood or decrease the energy levels in a room. Therefore, music can be used as a remote control to manage human behavior. An upbeat song can cause people to tap their feet, move from side to side, and most importantly, smile. Beginning a presentation with music to create positive energy in a room is genius. Playing music at appropriate times, such as while the audience members enter or leave a room, and while they are independently or collaboratively working, will trigger positive energy. If the goal is to create a happy atmosphere, then I recommend playing a song with a fast tempo at a high volume. Selecting the correct volume will make a difference. The entire song does not need to be played; hearing just a portion of a song can still make a positive impact.

It is also clever when the lyrics of the song choice directly relate to a message. This is another creative strategy that the presenter can utilize to reinforce the purpose of a speech. For instance, if I were giving a lesson about how our brains function optimally when we are in a positive state, I might play Bobby McFerrin's "Don't Worry Be Happy" as I am setting up my presentation. Educators have curated playlists and made them available online for presenters to consult.

Playing music at appropriate times throughout a speech and practicing the timing of the technology beforehand are keys to a successful presentation. Typically, I select songs for the beginning, middle, and end of my lessons, but sometimes, it might be appropriate to forego playing any songs in the middle of a talk if critical content must be delivered and time is limited. Starting a speech with a snippet of an upbeat song always promotes positive energy, so this is a practical tip when designing a presentation.

#InfuseHumor—Include a video or image to spark joy

If it is not appropriate to play music during a presentation, consider other methods to create a positive environment for learning. **The speaker does not have to be funny to spark joy** among the audience. Infusing humor at the beginning of the speech by utilizing a brief video clip or images, which make the audience smile or laugh, are feasible options. Given the plethora of free digital resources available online today, accessing such materials is extremely easy. Although setting a positive tone at the onset of a presentation seems trivial, it is actually a vital ingredient of a successful presentation. The goal is not just to make the audience laugh; it is to establish the optimal setting for learning.

#BePersonal—Engage in personal greetings and interactions

Giving a presentation is, in itself, a personal exchange of interactions and emotions. In his book, *Pedagogy of Freedom: Ethics, Democracy, and Civics of Courage*, Freire (1998) stated, "I cannot be a teacher without exposing who I am" (p. 77). If you take the human element out of the presentation, then you are simply reading your thoughts or delivering a paper. When possible, interact personally with your audience to add a personal approach to a presentation. Often, my students would enter my classroom without greeting me, and proceed to approach me solely with questions regarding their homework or a due date. In response, I stop, smile, greet them personally, and ask how they are doing. This usually makes them smile and brings us back to a courteous and more pleasant interchange. I believe that an audience will propagate what the presenter models, so if positive energy is being demonstrated, then it, too, will be multiplied.

The introduction is a critical part of a presentation because it will determine the audience's level of engagement and will set the tone for the entire speech. Neuroscientists and educators have confirmed that the brain thrives when it: (1) has purpose, and (2) resides in a positive state (Tate, 2016). Acknowledging these findings, presenters should make intentional efforts to develop introductions that include a clear purpose statement and create a positive setting for learning in order to maximize the learners' abilities to process, retain, and recall information. Including these fundamental steps when designing the introduction will lay a strong foundation for a successful presentation.

Content: How to Outline the Main Content of the Presentation

After the introduction is set, speakers must carefully think about how they will design the content of their presentations within the brief amount of time they are allotted. One important factor to consider is time. *If students were given 10 minutes to deliver a speech, then I would allow 2 minutes at the beginning for the introduction, 2 minutes at the end of the conclusion, and 6 minutes in the middle for the content.* Within the 6 minutes, if 3 main points were going to be explained, then each point would be allotted approximately 2 minutes. Dividing the time between the introduction, content, and conclusion is a practical first step when developing a presentation.

Once the timing has been established, presenters should embed the following three C's in their content: *(1) Chunking, (2) Comprehensible input, (3) Clues*. First, *chunking* will help break up the large bits of information that will be presented in the body of the presentation, and will assist the audience to digest the data more easily. Next, speakers must deliver the presentation with *comprehensible input*, or images and language that the class can easily understand, especially if it is a new topic and foreign to the audience. Lastly, it is helpful to incorporate *clues*, or memory strategies that are known as mnemonics to help the audience retain and recall the information that was shared. The following section will extrapolate on each of these elements further.

#Chunking—Break up the information into smaller bits

The information-processing model explains how the brain takes in data, retains it, and recalls it at a later time. Numerous studies completed on the brain's memory encoding abilities have found that data is more effectively encoded for understanding, retention, and retrieval when it is broken up into smaller bits, or chunks (Tate, 2016; Woolfolk, 2016). The common example of this is learning a phone number; the brain naturally separates the longer sequence of digits into smaller chunks, beginning with the area code, prefix of the number, and then, the last four digits in chunks of two sets. A random phone number such as 310-506-4000 could be broken down into 310, 506, 40, 00. Similarly, when giving a presentation, it is important to break down the content into a few key points and then to expand upon each of those main elements in the body of the presentation. Learners will be able to digest each point more easily, and this will add an element of organization and clarity to the presentation. Thus, if a presenter is talking about why college students should study abroad, the speaker should identify 2–3 main points that will be explained further in the body of the presentation. For example, studying abroad is a vital part of the collegiate experience, which: (1) promotes cultural appreciation, (2) allows students to connect their studies to real world artifacts such as travel sites and paintings, (3) fosters personal growth from travel experiences and living abroad. Listening to a presentation for a long amount of time while the presenter drones on about a single topic and does not break up the main body of knowledge into key points is particularly daunting. However, when these larger amounts of time are broken down into smaller chunks, and stimulating visuals and memorable hooks support the explanation of each main point, the likelihood for deeper learning increases.

#ComprehensibleInput—Use simple language that makes sense to the audience

Chunking information is important but can only truly be effective if the instructor presents the content in a manner that the audience can comprehend. This seems like a simple principle: **the presenter needs to make sense to the students.** However, it is appalling to observe how many university students I have witnessed who have been left dismayed in their college courses because they do not understand what their professors are saying. Many academic disciplines, and professional fields possess their own language, which include foreign acronyms that outsiders cannot decode. When we are so engrained in a culture, we forget that others do not share the same insider knowledge.

During graduation speeches or keynote addresses, I have watched noteworthy people, who have proven their success and expertise in a particular field, rant about their experiences using a foreign vernacular, which alienates their audiences. Speakers must be cognizant of their audience's background and construct a presentation that is meaningful to the learners. Comprehensible input increases the likelihood that the audience will learn something from the presentation and remember it too.

In my personal experiences, I have seen firsthand how learning can be impeded when comprehensible input is not provided. This was a common occurrence when I witnessed my husband trying to explain his work to others at dinner parties. When people asked my husband, who is a computer programmer, to explain his occupation, he routinely responded with a mechanical answer using technical jargon that is unfamiliar to the poor soul at the dinner party who was simply trying to initiate a pleasant conversation. My husband's original response included the following job description: "I program interfaces to financial switches, ATMs, and banking systems. We route financial transactions through various channels. We use C++ and COM+ objects for backend framework, and for the user interface we use ASP.NET, which is a programming paradigm, and C# for the development language." Later, I (gently) advised him to reconstruct his answer at these social gatherings so that people outside his area of expertise could understand his responses. Now, he simply answers, "I am a computer programmer. You know when you swipe your ATM card—well, I write computer programs that are needed behind the scenes to help carry out those transactions. Our company's programs allow banks and computers to talk to each other so that once a card is swiped, clients like you can get your money dispersed successfully." We made a lot more friends after my husband shared the second response. The key here is to use language that makes sense to the targeted audience. In order for the brain to encode data properly, the information must be meaningful, so providing comprehensible input is essential. You will make a lot more friends, or have more people interested in your presentation, if you adopt this helpful tip: **Use language that makes sense**.

#Mnemonics—Incorporate clues, or memory strategies

Mnemonics are memory strategies used to help the brain recall information easily. There are a wide variety of mnemonic techniques that have proven to be helpful in the teaching and learning process. When giving presentations, incorporating mnemonics can help the audience remember key points. The following section offers popular mnemonics that can be easily woven into presentations.

#Motions—Pair information learned with meaningful motions

One type of memory is muscle memory, or kinesthetic memory. Teaching the brain to associate movement in the learning process is a form of elaborative rehearsal that helps sear data into the long-term memory. In elementary school, hand motions associated with song and learning are common, yet this technique fades as students advance in their education. But, in my experience as a university professor, I have found some of my most successful student learning outcomes to be attributed to motions incorporated with my instruction. Marcia L. Tate (2016), author of *Worksheets Don't Grow Dendrites*, introduced me to this strategy, and I have applied it in my courses when teaching about the physiology of the brain in the learning unit that addresses cognitive psychology. Students hold up their hand and refer to it as a neuron, the basic unit of the brain. The fingers represent the dendrites, the palm symbolizes the cell body, and the forearm is referred to as the axon. As students point to the different parts of their hand, they elaborately rehearse the terminology of the brain. Though this method may seem elementary, it is effective and has empirically been proven to be successful.

Similarly, when I personally strive to remember something important, I attach a motion to it to insure that I will easily be able to recall the information. If the street name I must remember is Canoebrook Drive, then I will mimic paddling a canoe to sear the data into my long-term memory. Also, if I must recall where I have placed something, then I will turn to someone and share aloud where I have put the item, even if I know I will not see that person later. It is simply in executing this action of speech that will increase the brain's ability to recall the data at a later time. When giving a presentation, this strategy might translate into asking the audience to repeat a word in the speech in order to remember an important point.

#Images—Use powerful images

Images can serve as effective aids to trigger the memory. In a multimedia rich era, images can be found everywhere—on phones, tablets, digital marquees, computers, and movies. Pictures connect with the implicit memories of the brain, and effortlessly link memories to a visual symbol. Although presentations routinely include slides that are filled with text, it would benefit the audience more if the presenter simply used a powerful image to accompany the content of the speech. I have opened some of the professional talks I have given with projecting an image of a demure cat looking in a mirror at a reflection of a confident lion. I jokingly caution the audience not to measure my abilities by my petite size, given that I am only  about five feet tall. Pairing powerful images with the key points of a presentation helps audiences hang these central thoughts upon hooks found in the implicit memory sources of the brain.

As part of a culminating activity, college freshmen enrolled in my first-year seminar course are required to select an image and provide an explanation of how it represents their overall interpretation of educational research. I have seen slides filled with a variety of interesting images, such as Rubik's cubes, cats, children learning in a classroom, and an orchestra. The students appreciated and enjoyed this personal and creative exercise. They easily remembered the images as well as their explanations. Images are powerful and prime the long-term memory capacity of the brain.

#Acronyms—Create acronyms to recall key points of a presentation

Acronyms take initial letters of key terms to form nonsensical words that help the brain retrieve larger bodies of information. ROY G BIV was used to remember colors of the rainbow (red, orange, yellow, green, blue, indigo, violet), and IPMAT was used to recall the different phases of cell division (interphase, prophase, metaphase, anaphase, telophase). Heath and Heath (2007) applied this mnemonic in their book, *Made to Stick*. SUCCES (intentionally misspelled) helps readers to remember the key points of their book: Simple, Unexpected, Concrete, Credible, Emotional, Stories. I applied this strategy when I referred to the tips in designing the content of a presentation with the 3 C's: Chunking, Comprehensible Input, Clues. Even though the three C's do not produce a nonsensical word, they still help me to recall three tips that are explained in this section. If an acronym can be applied to help the audience remember the key points from the content of a presentation, it is a resourceful addition.

I have found that people's inclination is to go overboard when designing the content of a presentation. Presenters tend to write out full sentences on slides, use excessive text when creating visuals, and talk too much. The mantra "Less is more" applies here. ***Pull back a bit and use less text, apply large and powerful images, and say less***. Carefully consider each key point, its supporting evidence, and the hook you will use to sear this information into your audience's memory. These essential reminders will help you craft memorable content when delivering an effective presentation.

Conclusion: How to Finish Strong

The conclusion is a critical element in a presentation that is often overlooked. I cringe when I hear students close their presentations by saying, "And that's it," or "That's all I've got!" Instead, the end of a presentation should leave people with a summary of the main points of the presentation and a perplexing question or compelling thought that causes the audience to feel inspired or changed by the information that was shared. Imagine completing the gift of knowledge by tying the bow on top of the package, rather than leaving the bow untied. This vital step adds the final touch to finish strong when delivering a memorable presentation.

#Primacy-Recency Effect—State the key points at the beginning and the end

Sousa (2006), author of *How the Brain Learns,* has conducted extensive brain research and has found that the amount of information that an individual can retain is greatly influenced by the point in a presentation at which the material is presented. The brain's tendency to remember the most content delivered from the first and last part of a presentation, or even from a list information, is referred to as the primacy-recency effect. Humans remember best what came first and what came last. As the brain processes information, its attention is heightened at the beginning of a presentation, and then, proceeds to chunk or make sense of smaller bits of information throughout the instruction, and concludes with rehearsing the final points of a presentation in the last stage of the learning. Given these facts, it is important to reiterate the key points of a speech in the final moments of a presentation. The visual representation of this theory is analogous to an OREO cookie. The chocolate cookies sandwich the creamy contents, and in this same way, an effective presentation must demonstrate all three parts: (1) the introduction, (2) content, and (3) conclusion.

I have seen presenters engage their audiences effectively in their introductions and also follow the new instruction with thought-provoking examples. However, more often than not, the closing step of the presentation is forgotten. The presenter ends with a statement like, "Well, that's all I've got," or "That's all I have to say." These are cases where the presenter has surrendered the ability to take advantage of the second prime time of instruction for the brain to retain knowledge. The closure is a critical piece in the presentation that can be used to prompt audience members to leave a presentation rehearsing the main purpose of the instruction, thereby searing the data into their long-term memories and creating an unforgettable learning experience.

Conclusion

Public speaking is a valuable skill to learn and cultivate while in college. Opportunities to master the art of giving effective presentations will increase as a student, and in the future as an employee. This valuable skill will certainly set you apart in the classroom and in the workplace. The ability to deliver a strong, clear, organized, and dynamic presentation requires careful thought and intentional preparation. By considering the tips offered in this chapter, students can tap into the implicit memory skills of the brain and design a presentation that is both meaningful and memorable.

Research Summary

Discussion

1. How do you feel about giving public presentations?
2. Where does this confidence or fear come from?
3. How have you learned to design and execute presentations in the past?
4. What steps do you routinely follow when designing a presentation?
5. What strategies from this chapter do you wish presenters would implement more?

Application

1. Consider an occasion where you have found it easy to remember information, such as learning a song or a particular speech, and so on. Describe how you learned this information, and why you think it was so easy for your brain to retain and recall this information. How can this observation relate to the way you learn?
2. List five ways you could create a positive mood to begin a presentation. Include links, if applicable.
3. Describe a mnemonic or memory strategy that was used in a presentation you have seen that seared the content into your long-term memory.
4. Create five unique hashtags that summarize the presentation tips that you remember from this chapter.
5. Using presentation software, such as Powerpoint or Google Slides, create three slides to introduce yourself. First, use only text on each slide. Then, take those same three text-filled slides and create three new slides that only use images to convey the messages that were on your original slides. Attach a printout of the slides to these applications.

Additional Helpful Tips

1. Do not write text directly on a picture. Insert a grey rectangle and change the transparency.

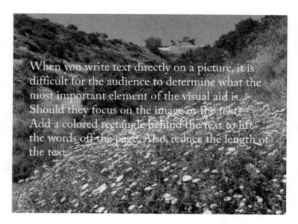

2. Do not read your slides. You tell the story. The slides are used to support what you are saying.

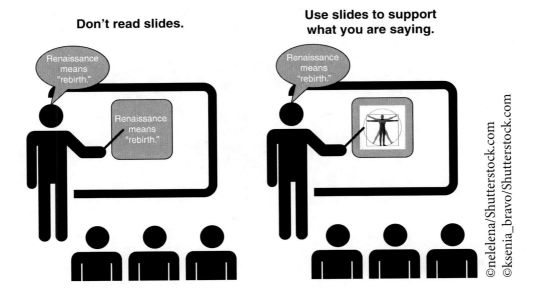

3. Do not use full sentences on a slide, unless it is displaying an important quote.

Music is one of the most underutilized tools when giving presentations. The tempo, rhythm, and beat of a song can help uplift a mood or decrease the energy levels in a room. Therefore, music can be used as a remote control to manage human behavior. An upbeat song can cause people to tap their feet, move from side to side, and most importantly, smile, so beginning a presentation with music to create positive energy in a room is genius.

"Music is one of the most underutilized tools when giving presentations."

CHAPTER 7

Technology

Managing Technology Responsibly in a Millennial World

"Technology is a useful servant but a dangerous master."

— *Christian Lous Lange*

Texting, Facebook, Instagram, Pinterest, Twitter, Snapchat—these are just a few of the most popular social outlets on mobile devices that students feel compelled to constantly check. Notifications grab people's attention and remind them to be socially connected all day long: *Someone you are interested in just texted you, a childhood friend sent a friend request, your friends posted a picture of themselves devouring the #besticecreamever, you need party decoration ideas for the next dorm social, a new hashtag is trending that says there is a celebrity sighting at your school, or your best friend from home sent you a Snapchat.* How can a college classroom compete with all of these distractions? How can students concentrate on taking notes in a lecture hall on sixteenth-century Renaissance art when their digital devices are calling for their attention in these stimulating ways? The struggle is real for college students. This chapter describes how technology has influenced this millennial generation and presents tips on how college students can manage technology responsibly.

The digital era

Freshmen entering college in 2017 were born around 1999. They have been frequently referred to as Millennials, Generation Y, or Digital Natives (Prensky, 2001). This generation grew up in a technologically rich world and does not recall a life without information and communication technologies (Junco, 2012). In fact, my youngest son was born early in the year 2000, and I recall when he received his first cell phone, a Verizon Cosmos, while in middle school. Other iconic digital inventions subsequently appeared in the 2000s, including *Facebook (2004), YouTube (2005), Twitter (2006), the first iPhone (2007), Instagram*

(2010), and Snapchat (2011). These digital tools are not simply an ordinary, external part of students' daily lives. Instead, cyborg anthropologist Amber Case (2010) proposed the idea that digital tools have become an extension of our physical bodies, and humans must daily maintain their physical selves as well as their virtual identities. Separating ourselves from technology now appears to be an odd and uncomfortable phenomenon. We feel incomplete and anxious without our mobile devices. As Case claims, *we are all cyborgs now.*

The prevalent use of technology among millennial college students is not surprising (Smith & Caruso, 2010); however, the digital distractions that mobile devices pose, both in and out of classrooms, are concerning (McCoy, 2016). Eagan, Stolzenberg, Ramirez, Aragon, Suchard, and Hurtado (2014) surveyed 153,015 first-time, full-time college students from 227 four-year U.S. college and universities and found that 27.2 percent of students spent more than six hours each week on social media, which has increased from 18.9 percent reported in 2007. Furthermore, 96 percent of all undergraduates own cell phones, and send an average of 97 text messages per day, with 71 of those messages being sent while doing homework (Junco & Cotten, 2012). It is clear that most college students possess digital devices and use them frequently, even in class. Nonacademic use of technology in learning settings is pervasive. McCoy (2013) surveyed 777 college students, and 85.9 percent reported texting during class. In another study completed with 675 college students from 26 states, 28.49 percent of respondents used a digital device for nonclassroom-related activities, from 4 to 10 times during class on a typical school day, while 21.51 percent used their devices for nonacademic purposes during class more than 11–30 times. *Texting (86.65%), email (76.18%), and social networking (70.26%) are the top three uses of digital devices for nonclass purposes* (McCoy, 2016). This is corroborated by the fact that within eight years, social media usage increased almost 1000 percent among the 18–29-year-old age group, who regularly check Facebook, Twitter, Pinterest, and Instagram (Duggan, 2015; Griffin, 2015). Ease of accessibility to digital devices and the Internet have made it feasible for increased technology usage for college students both in and out of the classroom.

Digital addiction

Our habitual use of technological devices has created an unhealthy dependency, or what some may call a digital addiction (Çagan, Ünsal, & Çelik, 2014; Roberts, Yaya, & Manolis, 2014). Humans have created this nonchemical addiction by constantly checking their mobile devices. Digital addicts check their smartphones more than 60 times per day, an increased rate of usage of 123 percent between 2013 and 2014 (Khalaf, 2014). Another study conducted by etextbook seller CourseSmart and Wakefield Research surveyed 500 college students and found that *38 percent could not go more than 10 minutes without checking a mobile device* (Kessler, 2011). Additionally, "41% feel moderately to highly anxious if they cannot check their text messages, and one in five feel the same if they can not connect with their social networks" (Rosen, Carrier, & Cheever, 2012, p. 956). Researchers argue that *the same neural networks reinforced by substance addiction are activated with the behavioral repetition of checking technological devices* (Roberts et al., 2014). Students feel a strong, consistent urge to communicate with friends via texting, instant messaging, and social media platforms. Although technological devices are also used for other utilitarian purposes, such as viewing the clock, browsing the news, or checking bank accounts, these applications have not been reported as the causes of digital addictions. Fostering social relationships and using the phone for entertainment purposes are the strongest predictors of addictive behavior (Roberts et al., 2014).

Technology rewires how the brain reads

Technology is slowly and implicitly changing how the brain reads. Before the Internet existed, students had to dedicate long periods of time to locate and comb through a myriad of references to identify key sources that pertained to their research. *The emergence of the Internet has conditioned the brain to skim texts quickly—like web pages.* Students seek hyperlinks for relevant information that is formatted in compact blocks (Taylor, 2012). This is why lengthy textbooks with single-line space formatting of endless text and no headings provided to scaffold the content leave readers feeling intimidated and overwhelmed. Carr (2010) equated reading books to the focused, quiet, and thoughtful exercise of scuba diving, while Internet reading is like the distracted, fast, and fleeting sport of jet skiing. This tendency to scan texts and only read bits of pertinent information makes reading textbooks unappealing for students and reduces their abilities to focus for long periods of time. As a result, it is difficult for college students to feel motivated to complete their long reading assignments and to sustain their attention during a class lecture for 1, 2, or 4 hours. The habitual tendency of switching from our main tasks to check our mobile devices and the ability to acquire information in brief formats, such as tweets, has negatively impacted students' attention spans and their reading habits (Carr, 2010; Junco, 2012; Junco & Cotten, 2012; Kuznekoff & Titsworth, 2013; McCoy, 2016; Rosen, Carrier, & Cheever, 2013; Taylor, 2012; Wood et al., 2012).

Technology changes teaching and learning

Technology has also changed the teaching and learning process. With universal access to the Internet, it is easy for students to locate basic facts and information instantaneously. *Classroom learning should move beyond the simple rote memorization of facts to cultivating critical thinking skills that can be applied to real-life problems.* This paradigm shift should cause faculty to rethink their instructional strategies, or pedagogy, because students can conceivably acquire the majority of lecture material from the Internet. The challenge for instructors is to update their language and pedagogy in a way that recognizes and connects with the thinking patterns of digital natives (Prensky, 2001). Adopting technology may pose a steep learning curve for many traditional teachers, but it must be confronted. Technology has changed the landscape of teaching and learning. Millennial students are skeptical of what they are learning in class and question why they are learning it. Digital natives know that they can and will access and apply information differently when they enter the workplace. Millennial students often ask themselves, "Why do I need to memorize this formula? Won't I be able to look it up or use a computer program to run the calculation for me when I am employed?" *Students see the incongruences between learning in the classroom and real-world applications.* In schools, students must move beyond the rudimentary levels of memorizing facts and be offered more opportunities to apply their problem-solving skills using authentic life scenarios. Learning how to communicate effectively in personal and professional contexts also needs to be addressed and practiced more. There is ample valuable instructional content that can replace the simple dissemination of information.

Technology promotes a multitasking generation

Technology has wired our brains to multitask. We have primed our brains to constantly be engaged and connected digitally. Even while waiting in line at a grocery store, people are engrossed with their phones. Because our tech-addictive behaviors reinforce the relentless need to check email, texts, instant messaging, and social platforms about every 10 minutes, it is difficult for our attention to be sustained by just one activity. Even if people are engaged in doing something pleasant, such as watching a television show or a movie, they will still check their mobile devices. It seems rare to see individuals focusing on only one task anymore. People regularly attend to two or more extraneous activities simultaneously. This process typically encompasses switching the brain's attention from one main task to a distracting function involving a mobile device.

Multitasking in classrooms

It is actually common to multitask in a classroom. The learning process usually engages students in two or more related activities at the same time—such as listening, processing information, and writing notes. However, the term *multitasking* has taken on a new connotation in light of this digital age as students can carry their personal mobile devices into classrooms. In this case, researchers who investigate students' abilities to multitask in academic contexts define *multitasking* as students' tendencies to divide their attention between two or more *unrelated* tasks while immersed in a learning context (Junco, 2012; Junco & Cotten, 2012; Wood, Zivcakova, Gentile, Archer, De Pasquale, & Nosko, 2012). A classic university scenario depicts students listening to a lecture in a college classroom or reading a textbook while simultaneously texting their friends or checking their social media accounts. Task switching, in this regard, impairs the brain's ability to process information. The ability for students to constantly divert their attention away from academic content impedes learning and detrimentally impacts educational outcomes (e.g., ***lower grades, longer time spent on academic tasks, missed instruction***).

Researchers have found that texting, emailing, and social networking are the top three nonacademic uses of technology in college classrooms (Bowman, Levine, Waite, & Gendron, 2010; Junco, 2012; Kuznekoff, Munz, & Titsworth, 2015; Roberts et al., 2014; Wood et al., 2012). A 2015 survey of 675 college students reported that respondents found it advantageous to use their digital devices in class to ***stay connected (63%), fight boredom (63%), and engage in entertainment (47%).*** Interestingly, the students surveyed also admitted that such behavior ***caused them not to pay attention (89%) and miss instruction (81%),*** but these negative effects did not deter them from using their mobile devices for nonacademic purposes in class (McCoy, 2016). This ability of students to check their mobile technologies, even while in class, reinforces the addictive behavior to stay digitally connected constantly.

What teachers can do—developing tech policies and updating pedagogy

How can a professor compete in sustaining students' attention while in class when they have the capability to communicate with all of their peers on their mobile devices? How can instructors leverage technology in a way that can enhance the learning process and engage millennial students? My purpose for including the following section in this book is to encourage students to share these ideas with their professors either directly (e.g., personal conversations) or indirectly (e.g., constructive feedback on course evaluations) so that faculty are aware of what students' needs are. In this way, changes can be made to improve course instruction.

Develop Technology Policies and Communicate Them Clearly to the Class

Technology has subtly crept into classrooms, and instructors are just now becoming aware that communicating a tech policy is necessary. As a result, a cultural norm has evolved in college classrooms where we see students open their laptops at the beginning of class to engage in academic and nonacademic tasks. It would be very beneficial for instructors to reflect upon how they would like to promote the responsible use of technology in their classrooms. College students have reported that it would be helpful to have a policy limiting nonclassroom use of digital devices (McCoy, 2016). I am not a proponent of restricting technology altogether, but I am an advocate of using digital tools for instructional purposes. *Teacher credibility is also increased when instructors communicate their tech policies to students*, and when teachers are able to explain the reason for their regulations (Finn & Ledbetter, 2013). Communicating clear expectations of appropriate technology usage is beneficial for all.

One suggestion is to foster the culture of using technological devices only when digital tools are necessary for learning activities. If time has been set aside for students to work collaboratively on a document or presentation or to pull up a particular learning tool from the Internet, then the use of technology is encouraged. My class policy is that students do not take notes using their laptops; instead, I encourage them to write their notes using pen, pencil, or colorful markers. After reviewing research on note taking and its connections to neuroscience, I am a strong believer that *students will retain more from the act of writing their notes versus recording statements using a word processor* (Makany, Kemp, & Dror, 2009; Tate, 2016; Willis, 2011). Students can take a picture of their notes afterwards and upload it to a cloud-based account, where they can access the image from anywhere at a later time. This strategy also reduces the likelihood of losing the notes.

I also take the time in class to talk about the responsible and respectful use of technology in the classroom. For me, I do not restrict cell phone use or texting using laptops, but I pause to discuss its appropriate use in our classroom community. This valuable discussion encourages students to be mindful of my technology policy as well as the appropriate use of mobile devices in my classroom. I have never witnessed nor would allow speaking on the phone during class, and texting is minimal. Students are also generally engaged in discussion or small group activities, which deters nonacademic technology usage. The idea here is that I am not policing how students use mobile devices; rather, we, as a community, have discussed the appropriate and respectful practices for our classroom.

Update Pedagogy

The emergence of the digital era has changed the way we learn, so it is logical to assume that technology would also directly impact teaching. Sadly, I see and hear about professors who restrict the use of digital devices in classrooms altogether to deter students from unproductive behavior. However, I do not think that having students put away their devices is the sole answer to the issue. Although I agree that students should practice appropriate uses of technology, I also believe that instructors should update their pedagogy. Faculty could benefit from learning how to optimize learning for digital students and investigating how technology could be harnessed in a useful way to motivate and engage the millennial generation (Gebre, Saroyan, & Bracewell, 2014; Sullivan, Johnson, Owen, & Conway, 2014). The responsibility lies not only with the students in learning how to manage digital tools responsibly, but also with the instructors in updating their pedagogy and appropriately addressing a digitally native generation (Prensky, 2001).

I recognize that it would be difficult for new college students to directly ask their professors to update their pedagogy. But, if students could add a constructive tip on a course evaluation that might encourage an instructor to adopt some new technologies, then this could benefit future classes. On a basic level, students could encourage faculty to post a syllabus online or insert more videos or images in a lecture. On more advanced levels, suggestions could be made for instructors to use a digital discussion board to promote further interaction or create a class wiki to synergize ideas on a given topic. It would also be helpful to recommend that instructors *divide their instruction into smaller, more manageable chunks of information to help sustain students' attention*. Rosen et al. (2012) proposed that technology breaks during large blocks of instructional time may aid in removing the internal distraction students will have to check their mobile devices. Knowing that there is a designated time to use technology for nonacademic purposes is a self-regulating strategy that may aid students to focus for a longer period of time. Faculty value constructive feedback, and these are helpful suggestions to positively impact instruction.

What students can do—use devices purposefully, turn off notifications and schedule tech breaks

Given that college students: (1) demonstrate addictive behavior in their technology usage, (2) exhibit short attention spans, and (3) tend to engage in nonacademic tasks while in academic settings, what can be done to improve their learning conditions? First, students must assess their cognitive abilities, and evaluate the optimal conditions in which they can study, think, and learn. The Career Center and Student Success Centers at universities offer learning style assessments if students choose to complete a formal evaluation. Otherwise, students can complete their own self-inventories and ask themselves questions such as the following:

- Do I study better alone or in groups?
- Do I need it to be silent or do I welcome a little noise or music while studying?
- What are the ideal hours for me to study?
- Do I learn material best when I write notes, listen to others, watch a video tutorial, or read information myself?

This is a good start to reflecting upon what you can do to monitor your own study habits. Then, they must discipline themselves to adopt effective techniques that will self-regulate their behavior so that they can maximize their ability to focus and process information.

Use Devices Purposefully

One simple metacognitive strategy is being mindful of using mobile devices purposefully while in class. Although it has become customary for students to open their laptops or tablets immediately after entering a classroom, I highly recommend that students not form this habit. Launching a digital device at the beginning of class opens the floodgates to distractions. This was confirmed earlier, when 89 percent of college students surveyed admitted that their digital devices detracted their attention in class (McCoy, 2016). Students know that the temptation to browse the Internet, read texts and emails, and check social media is just one click away. Digital devices are not the only tools that can be used to take notes in class; opting for the traditional method of note taking with pen and paper has greater benefits and is less distracting. Writing notes enhances long-term memory retention and supports information processing (Makany et al., 2009; Tate, 2016; Willis, 2011). *Using colored pens and markers* also sparks the imagination while note taking and reinforces ideas through highlighting important material and designing colorful concept maps. It would benefit students to take out their mobile devices only when the professors introduce an activity that requires a digital tool. Exercising this discipline to use technology purposefully in class will help students concentrate and will eliminate unnecessary diversions.

Turn Off Notifications and Texting Apps

Turning off social notifications and texting apps on mobile devices while in academic settings minimizes diversions. Students should not allow their phones to vibrate or light up during class or study sessions, because this will divert their attention from the educational task. Undergraduates should also remove the ability to text or chat with friends online when engaged in academic tasks. Studies clearly showed that these interruptions lead to missed instruction, longer time needed to process information, and lower academic performance (Bowman, et al., 2010; Junco, 2012; Junco & Cotten, 2011; Kuznekoff & Titsworth, 2013, Rosen, Lim, Carrier, & Cheever, 2011). Removing notifications on mobile devices and disabling texting apps on laptop computers are effective methods to maintain focus on the academic task at hand and increase learning.

Schedule Technology Breaks

Putting a cell phone away altogether is also another option, but Rosen et al. (2013) pointed out that "removing the external distraction does not remove the internal distraction" (p. 956). This is why scheduling technology breaks during study times, or even in class, will embed opportunities for students to quench their desire to check their mobile devices periodically. This metacognitive strategy also helps students to practice delayed gratification and to concentrate on one task without distractions. *Studies have found that alternating a 15-minute study period with a brief technology break increases attention, learning, and academic performance* (Rosen et al., 2013; Rosen et al., 2012). When I am working, my periods of focused work time typically last longer than 15 minutes, but this time frame is a good guideline. The idea is to concentrate for a continuous amount of time before checking a device, rather than repeatedly interrupting one's work. Implementing self-regulating strategies to help sustain attention and focus for blocks of time are needed to manage technology responsibly.

Conclusion

Technology has changed the way that we all live, think, and learn. Although digital tools provide many conveniences, they may also cause detrimental effects. Mobile devices have subtly entered our lives and quickly captured our attention, yet we have not paused to establish a cultural standard for technology usage. Instead, we are left tethered to our devices, no matter where we are or what we are doing. We are addicted to the satisfying feeling of constantly checking our phones, tablets, and computers. For students, the struggle to manage technology while navigating an academic world is genuine. The short attention spans of this digital generation and the urge to continually check their technological devices should be acknowledged. The key is for instructors and students to work together to model effective metacognitive strategies. This training will help young people develop appropriate habits of technology usage and practical self-regulating techniques to sustain their attention during the learning process.

Reflection Summary

Discussion

1. When do you recall getting your first cell phone, laptop, or tablet? How did this mobile device change your behavior?
2. Describe an occasion where you believe it is not appropriate to use a mobile device.
3. Name a show that you watch, or an activity that you engage in, that does not allow you to multitask. Explain why you are unable to multitask during this activity.
4. As a student, describe how technology has helped or hindered you.
5. What would your technology policy be as a classroom teacher?

Applications

Based on this 1–5 scale, mark a number next to the statement given:

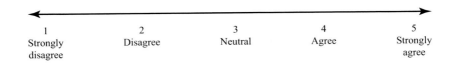

1	2	3	4	5
Strongly disagree	Disagree	Neutral	Agree	Strongly agree

SECTION I: Affective Influences

a. _____ I feel anxious when my professor says that technology is not allowed in class.

b. _____ It is distracting when I see other students engaged in nonacademic tasks on their computers in class.

c. _____ I feel like people think that I am technologically proficient when the truth is that I am not.

SECTION II: Academic Influences

d. _____ Technology is helpful to me as a student.

e. _____ I remember more when I take notes by hand versus on my computer.

SECTION III: Digital Influences

f. _____ I can function at my optimal level when multitasking in class.

g. _____ When I watch television, I usually have a mobile device out and multitask.

h. _____ I check my phone immediately after I wake up.

i. _____ I check my phone right before I go to bed.

j. _____ I am a tech addict.

SECTION IV: Instructor Influences

k. _____ My college professors apply digital tools innovatively in their teaching.

l. _____ My college professors use technology confidently in class.

m. _____ My college professors insert breaks in class time.

n. _____ My college professors introduce me to technology specific to their disciplines and interests.

o. _____ My college professors are willing to learn about technology from their students.

CHAPTER 8

Networking

Sowing the Seeds for Life after College

"Networking is more about 'farming' than it is about 'hunting'.
It's about cultivating relationships."

— *Dr. Ivan Misner*

Networking, or developing professional relationships, is a valuable skill that college students should practice early in their undergraduate careers. Forming meaningful connections with mentors, advisors, and peers who share like-minded values, interests, and goals, will support students as they pursue their university degrees and their professional careers. People often assume that networking is a skill that individuals exercise only after they are gainfully employed, but surrendering to this myth will not serve students well. The first life lesson for undergraduates in networking is to start early.

Experts in the field of college career services confirm that it is never too soon to begin networking. Researchers describe building professional connections as sowing the seeds before the harvest (Delgado, 2014; Doyle, 2016; Grant, 2011; Profina, 2016). Undergraduates can agree that the university application process suits this same metaphor. In order to be a competitive candidate for college admissions, students recall that a great deal of intentional planning took place prior to their senior year of high school. It would have been extremely challenging for students to develop a compelling profile that was worthy of college admission if they began the process in their final year of high school. In this same way, undergraduates must begin to build a professional network for moral support, recommendations, job referrals, wisdom, and advice immediately upon beginning their college careers. The end of college, especially, can be a perplexing time for students if they do not prepare adequately for the next step of their lives.

Students will reap the greatest benefits of networking if they invest time in developing meaningful friendships and not simply acquiring a myriad of superficial connections. The best networking comes from genuine relationships. Learning practical strategies to cultivate deeper connections would help this millennial generation, which has been reported to spend increasingly less time with friends and notably more time on social media (Eagan, Stolzenbery, Ramirez, Aragon, Suchard, & Hurtado, 2014). To begin, students should be personal and present when interacting with others. By maintaining eye contact, avoiding interruptions from mobile devices, listening attentively, and responding with relevant questions, students can foster genuine relationships. This chapter presents more suggestions for students to identify and develop valuable connections as they build their supportive networks.

Dual purposes for on-campus networking

Networking on-campus serves dual purposes. First, developing genuine relationships with people at the university can help students better navigate the new college community. There are numerous contexts in which to make connections while in college: resident halls, workplaces, general education classes, major courses, student clubs and organizations, study abroad programs, and more. Faculty, staff, and experienced students from these various settings can mentor and guide freshmen through stressful new experiences, such as registering for classes, deciding whether or not to participate in Greek life or international programs, and selecting a major. These valuable relationships can help answer new students' questions and offer them support through words of encouragement or even letters of recommendation. Additionally, the university campus provides an ideal setting for students to begin building professional connections in a discipline or industry in which they will study further or pursue work upon graduation.

Find a Faculty Mentor: Benefitting from Insider Knowledge and Expertise

One of the first tasks that I encourage my students to work on is finding a university faculty mentor. Students typically enter college with special advisors from their hometown community or former school, but it is particularly helpful for undergraduates to develop a close connection to a faculty mentor on their college campus. *A faculty mentor does not have to be a professor from one of your courses.* In fact, college students who are not registered in my classes have reached out to me via email after hearing me speak at a university event or after their friends have told them about my classes, my background, or my interests.

Professors are especially valuable resources because they can assist students with institutional procedures as well as life lessons. Having a faculty advocate is particularly beneficial when letters of recommendations are needed. Many colleges require students to obtain references from university faculty for scholarships, participation in special programs such as studying abroad or leadership positions in Greek life or the residential living community. Acquiring a thoughtful recommendation letter is difficult without developing a genuine relationship with a faculty mentor. Professors can likewise alert students to opportunities that they may not have known about otherwise, such as special internal scholarships, internships, or summer undergraduate research experiences. Having a personal resource on-campus to make you aware of this insider knowledge is extremely helpful. The role that faculty mentors can play in advising students and providing support, both personally and professionally, is invaluable.

New students may recognize the value of having a faculty mentor, but they might feel intimidated or may simply not know how to make the initial connection. Professors, while well educated, are people too; they generally enjoy spending time with and investing in students.

The following scenarios describe occasions when students have reached out to me to serve as their mentor and offer strategies for students to adopt to connect with faculty:

1. *Email after a School Retreat*: My university sponsored a special retreat to Catalina Island for sophomore students. I was invited to be the keynote speaker at the event. After the trip, one of the students who attended the trip sent me an email to ask if we could meet. She said that she could relate to my vocational story, which I shared during the retreat, and she wanted to discuss what impacted her from my talk. After meeting with her, she enrolled in one of my education classes as an elective. Although she did not pursue a degree in my discipline, I was still able to serve as her mentor by meeting with her frequently and advising her on her academic program and career choice. **Reach out to faculty via email. Schedule a time to initiate a deeper connection.**

2. *Email after University Chapel*: After serving on a faculty panel of female professors who talked about balancing work, motherhood, and marriage for a chapel series at my university, a female student emailed me and asked if we could meet. Again, the student said that the words I had shared during the presentation resonated with her, and she wanted to spend some more time speaking to me about finding balance in her life. I continued to correspond with her and to send her encouraging messages throughout her undergraduate career.

3. *Personal Ask from an Office Worker*: As I stood by the copy machine one morning in our division office, the student worker who I regularly greeted and chatted with paused to ask me if I might serve as her mentor in the Fulbright Scholarship application process. This entailed me assisting her in editing her essays and reviewing her application for the Fulbright Scholarship, which would allow her the prestigious opportunity to teach and conduct research in an international location such as Rwanda. This female student did not major in my discipline. We made a connection because she worked in my office, and we shared a mutual respect and admiration. The lesson here is that **continuous, informal connections with someone might inspire you to initiate a deeper relationship**. I was honored that this student personally requested me to be her Fulbright mentor, a role that allowed me to spend more intentional time with her. You do not need a formal project, such as a Fulbright application, to ask a professor to spend time with you. You simply need to ask.

4. *Personal and Electronic Requests from My Students*: Both male and female students from my classes have asked me in-person and via email to meet them for coffee, hold an office appointment, or share a meal with them. Our conversation topics range from academic advising, questions about career goals, and counseling about life lessons. Many of these appointments are held with students who have had me in a class in the past, and they continue to seek me out for wisdom or advice. This is an example of how students have fostered a meaningful relationship with a resource in their network.

These are just a few examples of how various students have reached out to me as a faculty mentor to help guide and support them while in college. Even after graduation, I continue to stay connected to many of my alumni. Our close connections are a product of the significant time we have purposefully invested to develop our meaningful relationships. Serving as a faculty mentor is an honor and a privilege that I consider to be a sweet fruit of my labor.

Develop Peer Networks: Spend Time Intentionally with Good People

Students have the potential to develop peer relationships in various contexts throughout a university campus. Resident halls, classes, workplaces, and clubs are all settings where students will meet new people. However, simply adding new acquaintances to a contact list is not the goal for networking. Instead, students should reflect upon what draws them to develop meaningful connections with certain peers, and they should consider how they will intentionally cultivate these relationships. The key to networking is to identify qualities in others that you admire, respect, or would like to emulate, and to purposefully invest in these connections. In other words, surround yourself with good people, and then, spend time intentionally with them.

I once invited a female college student in her senior year to be a guest speaker in my first-year seminar class. She advised the students about how to register for courses, and she also offered other insights into how to navigate college successfully. I selected her to speak in my class because she is recognized as an exceptional leader on my university campus, is actively engaged in student life, and she exhibits poise and professionalism beyond her years. She always makes those around her better, and the positive energy she exudes is inspiring. After she spoke, many freshmen remained after class to request her contact information so they could connect with her again later. They recognized the potential value of not only staying connected to this student leader, but also maintaining a close relationship with her. I always remind my students that many future leaders arise from college campuses. In this case, my guest speaker will move on to Harvard Graduate School, where she will study educational policy. I would not be surprised if she held a significant position in our nation's capitol one day. So, the students who followed up and invested further in this relationship were wise to do so. This is an example of intentionally developing a peer network.

The diverse contexts of college life will allow students to develop networks in various settings and for multiple purposes. Students may cultivate relationships with intellectual peers who support their academic work by serving as research partners, study group companions, or tutors. Developing close friendships with students who share common values or backgrounds also helps to build a personal support network. Fostering meaningful connections with peers who share the same career interests will add resources to a professional network. The university campus is filled with great potential to begin forming a robust network of resources.

Connect with University Administrators and Staff

Building connections with members of the university community is also greatly beneficial for students. Classes, student leadership opportunities, on-campus jobs, and special university events give students the opportunity to interact with administrators and staff. Cultivating these relationships and gaining the support of these key people during the college years can foster community, bolster confidence, and open opportunities. Letters of recommendations from the president or dean of a university will add great credibility and honor to a student's portfolio. This resource is particularly valuable for graduate school applications or future employment. Additionally, knowing staff members personally throughout campus can assist college students with questions regarding financial aid, academic programming, course registration, class wait lists, and student employment. Investing in relationships with university administrators and staff allows students to see personal connections throughout campus and adds valuable resources to their network.

Take Advantage of College Resources—Career Center and Alumni Office

Knowing how to begin networking can be particularly overwhelming for students if they are uncertain of their career direction and feel intimidated by initiating relationships. It benefits students to take advantage of services provided on-campus by the Career Center and the Alumni Office to help expand their connections and shape their professional profiles. Career Centers offer internship opportunities, personality assessments, résumé writing lessons, and interviewing workshops. Students can receive assistance and guidance from experts as they begin to build their professional identities. Many institutions also host career fairs, which are ideal occasions for students to speak personally with professionals, explore various openings, and establish connections. The Alumni Office is another valuable resource that students should contact to identify any graduates who work in a particular field of interest. Undergraduates could contact alumni regarding informational interviews, where they could learn more about a company or about potential internship opportunities. Often, undergraduates choose to attend a specific university because of its impressive alumni network. The university community works synergistically to support its students' futures, so students should take advantage of the services that the institution offers.

In my first-year seminar course about educational research, I invited a personal friend and graduate of my institution to be a guest speaker and share about his work as a college counselor. After the presentation, one of my students wanted to learn more about his work and the pathway to follow to be a college counselor, so she followed up with him and visited his school. Typically, alumni display a loyal allegiance to their university and want to help guide a new generation of students. In this case, the undergraduate was able to spend some time shadowing the alumnus, which gave her a better understanding of the work of a college counselor.

Cultivate relationships off-campus

It is equally important for college students to cultivate relationships with people off-campus for networking purposes. Tapping into the resources of family members, personal contacts, and employers is useful when building one's professional network. Students will also independently grow their connections during their college years as they travel and assume summer employment opportunities. Identifying ways to expand one's network through opportunities off-campus should not be overlooked.

Conduct Informational Interviews

Informational interviews provide an ideal opportunity for students to meet with professionals to learn more about their careers. Undergraduates can tap into the networks of their personal contacts, friends' referrals, and alumni of their institution for suggestions of people who represent their job-related interests. Students should arrive at the interview professionally dressed and prepared with questions to ask the professional. During the interview, students can inquire about the pathway that the individual traversed to obtain their position, as well as any details relevant to the work. Informational interviews allow students to take the first step in purposefully networking in a career field that greatly interests them. For many, this connection can transpire into an internship or employment in the future.

Travel Extensively: Make International and Domestic Connections

The college years present an ideal time for domestic and international travel. Being unrestricted by the responsibilities of a salaried position, home ownership, or a family of their own, most undergraduates have the freedom to travel extensively during summer, long breaks, and weekends. Additionally, study abroad programs allow college students to explore the world while simultaneously pursuing their undergraduate degrees. Given these special circumstances, I highly encourage undergraduates to take advantage of this unique time in their lives and travel as much as possible. During their travels, students will meet interesting people and make connections. Cultivating these relationships will grow students' professional networks extensively at an international and domestic level.

A female education student from my university spent her spring break participating in a service project in Fiji, where she taught kindergarten and assisted teachers in underprivileged areas. After the experience was concluded, she continued to stay connected to the leader of the project and further researched the dilemma of accessing modern curriculum in rural settings. Years later, the student is finishing a doctorate in education, and she will return to Fiji for data collection. The idea for the project and her love for the students were realized through her travels to Fiji and the special connection she maintained with the project leader. This is an example of how a traveling experience in college evolved into a larger opportunity through networking efforts.

Spend Summer Months Intentionally: Summer Employment and Internships

The summer months offer an excellent opportunity for college students to pursue employment or internships that can help them intentionally explore their professional interests. Many colleges provide summer undergraduate research experiences for students to engage fully in original projects alongside a faculty mentor. Some of these programs compensate students for their work, while others are unpaid positions that may award course credits. Undergraduates should also explore practicums in their field of interest, such as working for a news station, interning at the White House, or clerking for a law office. It is important for students to be intentional about how they will spend their summer months, because this is an ideal time that can be used to build a résumé and expand networks in preparation for the next step after graduation.

Create networking materials: Résumé, business cards, and professional images

As students build their professional networks, they will find it useful to create some essential materials that will come in handy when making connections. A detailed résumé, a well-designed and informative business card, some professional images, and a clean, digital presence are all practical resources that are worth developing. Having these tools readily accessible shows others that you are polished and prepared to add them to your network. Networking is based largely on not only making connections, but also following up with individuals after initially meeting them. Providing websites, business cards, and résumés for people increases the number of tools that people can use to remember you and reconnect with you later.

Build a Detailed Résumé

A résumé is one essential tool necessary to engage in the networking process. Potential employers, personal contacts, and faculty mentors are just a few people who may request a résumé from students. The purposes for a résumé request may include, but are not limited to, potential employment, job referral, scholarship application, and letter of recommendation. The following tips are helpful as students compose a detailed résumé:

1. *Include activities mainly from your college years.* Unless students have made significant contributions in their lives prior to college, their résumés should solely reflect their education, activities, and accolades from their undergraduate careers. It is helpful for students to keep a running list of their involvements and achievements in college so that nothing is mistakenly omitted from a résumé. Developing a résumé early on in college prompts students to thoughtfully consider how they will purposefully spend their time and shape their professional profile.

2. *Use key words and vivid descriptions.* Students should utilize keywords that search engines or résumé program scanners will identify when reviewing a résumé for particular positions. For instance, terms such as "innovator, learning designer, collaborator, and curator" are relevant for employment in educational technology. The use of active verbs and vivid descriptions is also essential in portraying the unique elements of a position or activity to clearly explain the unique nature of the work to the reader. An "instructional assistant" may be a vague term, but if it is followed up with descriptors such as "carried out reading assessments with 20-first-graders; documented data; created intervention plans for students reading below grade level," then a more vivid picture of the work is painted.

3. *Create a cohesive* résumé. Students should be mindful of creating a cohesive résumé that effectively represents their professional identity. So, if students are interested in journalism, then their résumés should not include a server position for a restaurant held during a random summer. Instead, students should highlight their research, presentation, and technological skills that will convince the potential employer that they are suitable

for the position. Job announcements will typically provide a detailed description that applicants should read carefully. It would benefit students to highlight those qualities or experiences they possess which are outlined in the job description. Often, this will cause applicants to write customized cover letters for different positions or to reformat a résumé to draw attention to relevant work. This is completely understandable so that you can represent yourself in the best way possible given the descriptions that the companies have outlined.

4. *Design an imaginative résumé using infographics.* Some résumés have taken on creative design layouts with the application of infographics. (See appendix for creative résumé example.) Although this is a unique approach to résumé writing, some conservative companies may still appreciate a traditional format. Therefore, it may be helpful to maintain a traditional résumé, and then to create an additional document that applies imaginative possibilities using more graphic designs. It is ultimately left to the discretion of the applicant to decide which résumé to submit to an employer, unless the employer requires a particular format. If applicants are uncertain and providing both a traditional and nontraditional résumé does not appear excessive, then this might be a viable option.

5. *Link your résumé on a professional website.* A detailed résumé can be made available on a student's professional website. Posting the résumé on a webpage will allow students to broaden their network and accessibility. Sharing it with a school's career center website will also expand possibilities to connect with professionals.

Carry a Business Card

College students meet people and make connections at formal and informal gatherings everywhere. Networking opportunities arise in planned and unplanned events, so it is always best that students are prepared. A professional method to share contact information is handing a new acquaintance a business card. This strategy allows students to offer recipients a memorable and tangible tool to help them reconnect and begin building a meaningful relationship. Students can design their own cards using their computers, or they can select a company online and apply a pre-made template. Pertinent information includes a student's full name, phone number, and email address. Extraneous content may include a special quote, students' general interests or talents, or employment objective. Business cards are affordable, useful tools that make students look polished and prepared when networking.

Create a Database of Professional Profile Images

For applications, email accounts, or projects, it is often necessary to upload or post a professional profile image. It is very helpful to have a folder full of at least five updated pictures that students can use for networking purposes. The images look best if the person is not simply cropped out of a group picture. An assortment of professional pictures can be taken simply using a Smart phone. A range of black and white, color, full-body, and portrait settings should be considered. Having this database of images will be a practical tool that can be easily accessed when developing one's professional identity.

Be Mindful of How Technology Can Help or Hinder Professional Opportunities

In today's digital age, students should recognize how technology can both help and hinder their professional networking opportunities. The ability to join professional networks online through social media platforms, such as Facebook, Twitter, and LinkedIn, can exponentially increase students' connections. The Internet also allows students to research employment opportunities and to locate contact information of key people who they can connect with directly regarding specific positions. Students' abilities to network have expanded significantly because of technology.

On the contrary, students must be mindful of their digital footprint and the detrimental effect it can have. According to a survey conducted by CareerBuilder in 2016, *60 percent of hiring managers use social media to screen job applicants*. Although most administrators cited that their objective when looking at social media accounts was to find evidence that the candidates were qualified for a particular job, *49 percent reported that they found information that caused them not to hire an applicant*. This content ranged from inappropriate photographs, drug or alcohol usage, negative comments about a previous employer, and poor communication skills. Like Case (2010) suggests, people must maintain not only their physical selves, but also their digital selves. Students must carefully consider how their digital posts will shape their professional identities.

Conclusion

Networking is an enriching and enjoyable experience because it helps individuals identify and connect with key people who will play significant roles in their lives. Members of the professional networks that I have fostered support my work, expose me to new opportunities, and guide my next steps. These are valuable relationships that I have intentionally invested in and that have blessed me personally and professionally. My hope is that students reading this chapter will also realize the potential of networking and take purposeful steps in cultivating their own connections.

Reflection Summary

Discussion

1. Look back upon your high school experience. How were you intentional about networking to prepare your college application?
2. What are some activities you definitely want to participate in while in college? How could these opportunities help you with resources for the next step in your life after college?
3. Describe a mentor you have had in your past. How did this individual play a significant role in your life, and how did you find him/her? (Use nonfamily members as examples.)

Applications:

1. Take five professional profile images of yourself. Be sure to set them up differently: black and white, color, portrait, landscape, full-body, half-body, face only.
2. Design a business card for yourself. Include your name, title, interests, contact information, and special quote or motto.
3. For the list of the following items, write 0 = Not going to do it, 1 = Definitely going to do it, 2 = May do it. Be prepared to explain your answers in class.

   a. _____ Study abroad for at least a semester.
   b. _____ Create a professional Twitter account.
   c. _____ Visit the Career Center.
   d. _____ Directly email a professional that you do not know.
   e. _____ Join a student club.
   f. _____ Join an academic honor society.
   g. _____ Contact the Director of the Alumni Association.
   h. _____ Ask other college students about university professors.
   i. _____ Include infographics for your professional résumé.
   j. _____ Create a LinkedIn profile.
   k. _____ Conduct an informational interview with someone in your chosen career field.
   l. _____ Get a job in the field that you are interested in pursuing after graduation.
   m. _____ Complete an internship.

Conclusion

The college years are not simply about grades. They are about growth. This critical time in young people's lives launches them into independence and initiates a journey of transformative life lessons that overshadows the academic curriculum. Equipping undergraduates with practical advice to support their adult development is a need that I uncovered after working closely with college students. I have witnessed firsthand how teaching the life skills outlined in this book increases students' confidence and self-efficacy in classrooms, as well as in personal and professional settings. This text makes visible to students the unwritten course of life lessons encountered in college.

In the book, *The Defining Decade: Why Your Twenties Matter – And How to Make the Most of Them Now*, Jay (2013) confirmed that the majority of life's consequential experiences take place in people's twenties. The author found:

> Eighty percent of life's most defining moments take place by age thirty-five. Two-thirds of lifetime wage growth happens in the first ten years of a career. More than half of us are married, or dating, or living with our future partner, by age thirty. Personality changes more during our twenties than at any time before or after. The brain caps off its last growth spurt in the twenties. (p. xiv)

Looking back on my own experiences, I see how these transformative years laid the foundation for my professional networks, marked the beginning of my marriage and family, launched me into my career, helped expand my worldview, and shaped my beliefs. Although I did not realize it at the time, my college years initiated a defining decade in my life.

My experiences = Life lessons

The prominent life lessons that I learned as a college student, and continuously witness as a college professor, formed the chapters of this book. My personal growth in college began with basic steps such as selecting a major (Chapter 1). This might seem like a simple task, but in reality, it is not. Such a decision involves a great deal of deep, introspective reflection. I asked myself questions such as: Is this what I want, or is this what my parents want? Will this decision bring me joy? Will this major serve me well if I decide to change professions? How will I explain my decision to my parents? Experiences like these began to shape me as a college student, and these decisions ultimately impacted my future.

Living on my own for the first time in an unfamiliar setting filled with domestic and international students also obliterated my narrow view of the world. After moving into my first college dormitory, I recall being amazed by how far people had traveled to attend the university, which was only one hour from my home. Being separated from my family and introduced to a wide array of students from all over the world truly enlightened my understanding of people (Chapter 2). My worldview expanded after being exposed to diverse places, personalities, upbringings, cultures, and living habits.

Knowing how to communicate with others (Chapter 3) is a skill that proves to be valuable in both personal and professional contexts. Writing Thank You notes, interacting with university professors, and resolving difficulties with roommates or peers are important lessons that my students appreciate learning. Understanding my audience, selecting words carefully, and conveying an accurate tone in my messages are key elements in the communication process that I continue to apply in my adult life as I meet different people and form new relationships.

After reflecting upon my own undergraduate experiences, I curated a list of skills that would be helpful for students to develop while in college. My direct work with undergraduates also confirmed the relevance and need to emphasize these essential life practices. Managing my time appropriately (Chapter 4) was a foundational piece of my college puzzle, which facilitated the ease with which I completed all of my responsibilities. Preserving my mental wellness (Chapter 5) was key in helping me function at my optimal level. Professional practices, including how to design and deliver memorable presentations (Chapter 6), adopting appropriate uses of technology (Chapter 7), and cultivating connections to build my professional network (Chapter 8), shaped my work ethic and professional identity. These life skills were not cultivated from formal class assignments. Instead, they were lessons that were presented throughout my overall university experience. This was the unwritten course of college that taught me practical knowledge, which I continue to use throughout my life.

Be a torchbearer: Share your light with others

William Butler Yeats wrote, "Education is not the filling of a pail, but the lighting of a fire." As a teacher, I imagine my role in education to be much like the function of a torchbearer. Through my work with students, I make efforts to ignite their passions and illuminate the pathways to their futures. My desire is for this book to be a spark of inspiration, encouragement, or knowledge for students as they navigate their college journeys. When the path appears dark or uncertain, my hope is that this book will offer strategies that will illuminate your next steps. In turn, if you find a particular tip to be exceptionally helpful, then I encourage you to share it with others, thus extending the light that we have shared.

You've got this!

The college years mark a unique, transformational time in your lives that can rarely be duplicated. As undergraduates, you still maintain some childlike freedoms and optimistic worldviews, but you also make adult decisions that will impact the trajectory of your futures. With the practical tips offered in this text, and the support of mentors, family, and friends, I am confident that you will be sufficiently prepared (and definitely more prepared than I was) to thrive as a college student and transition seamlessly into adulthood.

One of my goals for this book was to encourage students as they grappled with succeeding in rigorous university classes and balancing the complexities of adult development. Throughout life, and especially during college, I believe that everyone needs a cheerleader. My hope is that through this book, I have been able to serve as yours in some small way. When life lessons challenge you and you think you have lost your way, I hope that you can open this text and feel empowered with knowledge, equipped with tools, and encouraged by my words. I leave you now with my family's parting mantra and my final cheer for you: *Make good choices! Don't do drugs! Stay in school!* Sleep! Manage your time purposefully! Surround yourself with good people! Study hard! Enjoy the journey! You've got this.

Works Cited

Achor, S. (2011, May). *The happy secret to better work*. Retrieved from http://www.ted.com/talks/shawn_achor_the_happy_secret_to_better_work

American College Health Association. (2016). *American College Health Association-National College Health Assessment II: Undergraduate student reference group executive summary spring 2016*. Hanover, MD: American College Health Association.

Ault, J. T., & Barney, S. T. (2007, March). Construct validity and reliability of Hartman's Color Code Personality Profile. *International Journal of Selection and Assessment, 15,* 72–81.

Baltz, J. (2016, April 4). *Is sleep deprivation the new college norm?* Retrieved from http://www.huffingtonpost.com/jacqueline-baltz/sleep-deprivation-the-norm-college_b_9586402.html

Bowman, L. L., Levine, L. E., Waite, B. M., & Gendron, M. (2010). Can students really multitask? An experimental study of instant messaging while reading. *Computers & Education, 54,* 927–931.

Budig, G., & Heaps, A. (2013, August 7). *Are we in the middle of a writing revolution?* Retrieved from http://www.usatoday.com/story/opinion/2013/08/07/writing-revolution-digital-technology-column/2621353/

Buechner, F. (1993). *Wishful thinking: A seeker's ABC*. San Francisco, CA: HarperSanFrancisco.

Çagan, Ö., Ünsal, A., & Çelik, N. (2014). Evaluation of college students' level of addiction to cellular phone and investigation on the relationship between the addiction and level of depression. *Procedia Social and Behavioral Sciences, 114,* 831–839.

Cain, S. (2012). *Quiet: The power of introverts in a world that can't stop talking*. New York, NY: Crown Publishers.

CareerBuilder. (2016). Retrieved from http://www.careerbuilder.com/share/aboutus/pressreleasesdetail.aspx?ed=12/31/2016&id=pr945&sd=4/28/2016

Carr, N. (2010). *The shallows: What the Internet is doing to our brains*. New York, NY: W.W. Norton & Company Ltd.

Case, A. (2010). *We are all cyborgs now*. Retrieved from https://www.ted.com/talks/amber_case_we_are_all_cyborgs_now#t-451674

Chapman, G. D. (1995). *The five love languages: How to express heartfelt commitment to your mate*. Chicago, IL: Northfield Pub.

Chowdhry, A. (2013, April 24). *12 tips for increasing productivity*. Retrieved from https://www.forbes.com/sites/amitchowdhry/2013/04/24/12-tips-for-increasing-productivity/#4e59f04246de

Coleman, J. (2013, April 5). Handwritten notes are a rare commodity. They are also more important than ever. *Harvard Business Review*. Retrieved from https://hbr.org/2013/04/handwritten-notes-are-a-rare-c

Duggan, M. (2015, August 19). *Mobile messaging and social media 2015*. Retrieved from http://www.pewinternet.org/2015/08/19/mobile-messaging-and-social-media-2015/

Eagan, K., Stolzenberg, E. B., Ramirez, J. J., Aragon, M. C., Suchard, M. R., & Hurtado, S. (2014). *The American freshman: National norms fall 2014*. Los Angeles, CA: Higher Education Research Institute, UCLA.

Everday Thomist. (2010, January 25). *What Malcolm Gladwell's Blink teaches about virtue*. Retrieved from https://everydaythomist.wordpress.com/2010/01/25/what-malcolm-gladwells-blink-teaches-about-virtue/

Finn, A. N., & Ledbetter, A. M. (2013, January). Teacher power mediates the effects of technology policies on teacher credibility. *Communication Education, 62*, 26–47.

Freire, P. (1998). *Pedagogy of freedom: Ethics, democracy, and civic courage*. Maryland, MD: Rowman and Littlefield Publishers.

Gebre, E., Saroyan, A., & Bracewell, R. (2014). Students' engagement in technology rich classrooms and its relationship to professors' conceptions of effective teaching. *British Journal of Educational Technology, 45*, 83–96.

Gladwell, M. (2017). *Why do we love tall men?* Retrieved from http://gladwell.com/blink/why-do-we-love-tall-men/

Gladwell, M. (2005). *Blink: The power of thinking without thinking*. New York, NY: Little, Brown and Company.

Gladwell, M. (2002, January). *The tipping point: How little things can make a big difference*. New York, NY: Little, Brown and Company.

Griffin, R. (2015). *Social media is changing how college students deal with mental health, for better or worse*. Retrieved from http://www.huffingtonpost.com/entry/social-media-college-mental-health_us_55ae6649e4b08f57d5d28845

Heath, C., & Heath, D. (2007). *Made to stick: Why some ideas survive and others die*. New York, NY: Random House.

Hensher, P. (2012, December 29). The lost art of the handwritten note. *Wall Street Journal*. New York, NY: Dow Jones & Company, Inc.

Hershner, S. D., & Chervin, R. D. (2014) Causes and consequence of sleepiness among college students. *Nature and Science of Sleep, 6*, 73–84.

Jay, M. (2013). *The defining decade: Why your twenties matter – and how to make the most of them now*. New York, NY: Hachette Book Group.

Junco, R. (2012). In-class multitasking and academic performance. *Computers in Human Behavior, 28*, 2236–2243.

Junco, R., & Cotten, S. R. (2012). No A 4 U: The relationship between multitasking and academic performance. *Computers & Education, 59*, 505–514.

Kessler, S. (2011). *38% of college students can't go 10 minutes without tech [STATS]*. Mashable Tech. Retrieved from http://mashable.com/2011/05/31/college-tech-device-stats/

Khalaf, S. (2014, April 22). *The rise of the mobile addict*. Retrieved from http://urrymobile.tumblr.com/post/115191945655/the-rise-of-the-mobile-addict

Kuznekoff, J. H., Munz, S., & Titsworth, S. (2015). Mobile phones in the classroom: Examining the effects of texting, Twitter, and message content on student learning. *Communication Education, 64*, 344–365.

Kuznekoff, J. H., & Titsworth, S. (2013). The impact of mobile phone usage on student learning. *Communication Education, 62*, 233–252.

Lee, H. (1960). *To kill a mockingbird*. New York, NY: Hachette Group USA.

Lenz, S. A. (2014, October). Mediating effects of relationship with mentors on college adjustment. *Journal of College Counseling, 17*, 195–207.

Makany, T., Kemp, J., & Dror, I. E. (2009). Optimising the use of note-taking as an external cognitive aid for increasing learning. *British Journal of Educational Technology, 40,* 619–635.

Mayberry, M. *(2015, January 1). 5 daily habits that will increase your productivity levels. Retrieved from* https://www.entrepreneur.com/article/241797

McCoy, B. R. (2013, October). Digital distractions in the classroom: Student classroom use of digital devices for non-class related purposes. *Journal of Media Education, 4,* 5–14.

McCoy, B. R. (2016, January). Digital distractions in the classroom phase II: Student classroom use of digital devices for non-class related purposes. *Journal of Media Education, 7,* 5–32.

McGuire, G., & Reger, J. (2003). Feminist co-mentoring: A model of academic professional development. *NWSA Journal, 15,* 54–72.

Mistler, B. J., Reetz, D. R., Krylowicz, B., & Barr, V. (2012). *The Association for University and College Counseling Center Directors (AAUCCD) Annual Survey Report.*

The Myers & Briggs Foundation. (2014). *MBTI Basics.* Retrieved March 20, 2017, from http://www.myersbriggs.org/my-mbti-personality-type/mbti-basics/

Palmer, P. (2000). *Let your life speak: Listening for the voice of vocation.* San Francisco, CA: Jossey-Bass.

Petersen, A. (2016, October 16). Students flood college mental-health centers. *Wall Street Journal.* Retrieved from https://www.wsj.com/articles/students-flood-college-mental-health-centers-1476120902

Prensky, M. (2001, October). Digital natives, digital immigrants. *On the Horizon, 9,* 1–6.

Radicati, S. (2014, April). *Email Statistics Report, 2014-2018.* Palo Alto, CA: The Radicati Group, Inc.

Ramos, Y. (2013). *College students tend to change majors when they find the one they really love.* Retrieved from http://borderzine.com/2013/03/college-students-tend-to-change-majors-when-they-find-the-one-they-really-love/

Reilly, K. (2017). *Read what Michelle Obama said in her final remarks as first lady.* Retrieved from http://time.com/4626283/michelle-obama-final-remarks-transcript/

Roberts, J. A., Yaya, L. H. P., & Manolis, C. (2014). The invisible addiction: Cell-phone activities and addiction among male and female college students. *Journal of Behavioral Addictions, 3,* 254–265.

Rosen, L. D., & Carrier, L. M., & Cheever, N. A. (2013). Facebook and texting made me do it: Media-induced task-switching while studying. *Computers in Human Behavior, 29,* 948–958.

Rosen, L. D., Cheever, N. A., & Carrier, L. M. (2012). *iDisorder: Understanding our obsession with technology and overcoming its hold on us.* New York, NY: Palgrave Macmillan.

Rosen, L. D., Lim, A. F., Carrier, L. M., & Cheever, N. A. (2011). An examination of the educational impact of text message-induced task switching in the classroom: Educational implications and strategies to enhance learning. *Psicologia Educative (Spanish Journal of Educational Psychology), 17,* 163–177.

Rosen, L. D., Whaling, K., Rab, S., Carrier, L. M., & Cheever, N. A. (2012). Is Facebook creating "iDisorders"? The link between clinical symptoms of psychiatric disorders and technology use, attitudes and anxiety. *Computers in Human Behavior, 29,* 1243–1254.

Skierkowski, D., & Wood, R. M. (2012). To text or not to text? The importance of text messaging among college-aged youth. *Computers in Human Behavior, 28,* 744–756.

Smith, S. D., & Caruso, J. B. (2010). *The ECAR study of undergraduate students and information technology.* Boulder, CO: EDUCAUSE. Retrieved from http://www.educause.edu/Resources/ECARStudyofUndergraduateStudent/217333

Sousa, D. A. (2006). *How the brain learns.* Thousand Oaks, CA: Corwin Press.

Straumsheim, C. (2016, March 2). *Read and unread*. Retrieved from https://www.insidehighered.com/news/2016/03/02/study-explores-impact-social-media-texting-email-use

Sullivan, A., Johnson, B., Owens, L., & Conway, R. (2014). Punish them or engage them? Teachers' views of unproductive student behaviours in the classroom. *Australian Journal of Teacher Education, 39,* 43-56.

Tate, M. L. (2016). *Worksheets don't grow dendrites: 20 instructional strategies that engage the brain (3rd ed.)*. Thousand Oaks, CA: Sage Publications Ltd.

Taylor, J. (2012, December 4). *How technology is changing the way children think and focus*. Retrieved from https://www.psychologytoday.com/blog/the-power-prime/201212/how-technology-is-changing-the-way-children-think-and-focus

Trebay, G. (2014, April 4). *The found art of thank-you notes*. Retrieved from https://www.nytimes.com/2014/04/06/fashion/the-found-art-of-thank-you-notes.html?_r=1

U.S. Department of Commerce. (2015, August). *Census Bureau, Current Population Survey (CPS), October, 1970 through 2014*. Retrieved from https://nces.ed.gov/fastfacts/display.asp?id=372

Wapnick, E. (2015, April). *Why some of us don't have one true calling*. Retrieved from https://www.ted.com/talks/emilie_wapnick_why_some_of_us_don_t_have_one_true_calling

Willis, J. (2011, May 3). *Writing and the brain: Neuroscience shows the pathways to learning*. Retrieved from http://www.nwp.org/cs/public/print/resource/3555

Wood, E., Zivcakova, L., Gentile, P., Archer, K., De Pasquale, D., & Nosko, A. (2012). Examining the impact of off-task multi-tasking with technology on real-time classroom learning. *Computers & Education, 58,* 365-374.

Woolfolk, A. (2016). *Educational psychology (13th ed.)*. Boston, MA: Allyn & Bacon.

MS. TEACHER
History Teacher

EDUCATION

MASTER OF ARTS IN EDUCATION
Best University
2011

BACHELOR OF ARTS IN HISTORY
Great University
2007

CERTIFICATION

CALIFORNIA CLEAR CREDENTIAL
Social Studies - 2013

SKILLS

Microsoft Office

Canvas LMS

Blackbaud

SMART Board

CONTACT

 ###-###-####

 MYemail@gmail.com

 MYwebsite.com

ABOUT ME

I am driven by my love of history, and making it come alive for teenagers. As a teacher I see it as one of my greatest duties to instill in my students a love of learning and a sense of wonder about our world. While history may be the study of the past it is vital that I help students make connections between the past and the 21st century, whether by analyzing direct causes and correlations to current events or timeless thematic parallels and lessons about human nature.

TEACHING EXPERIENCE

A HIGH SCHOOL - SOMEWHERE, CA
Teacher – 10th grade modern European history & 11th grade U.S. history
August 2011 – Present

- Integrated primary sources, art styles, digital media in daily curriculum
- Created video lectures for student use when absent or for independent review, implemented by other faculty
- Worked on-one-on with students to develop individualized note-taking skills and study methods
- Collaborated with members of history department to develop simulation activities for students to experience specific historic events, concepts
- Planned and led educational student trips to Europe to trace events Second World ar, history of British Empire

PERSONAL INTERESTS

Contestant on
JEOPARDY! in 2006

Reading. Lots of
reading

Cooking for friends
& family

International travel to
Europe & Africa

Played handbells, directed
choir in Washington D.C.